Missionaries, Parents and Girls who wait

David R. Mickel

©1983 by Randall Book
All rights reserved.
International Standard Book Number
0-934126-34-8

First Printing April 1983

Randall Book
Orem, Utah
Printed in the United States of America
Publishers Press
Salt Lake City, Utah

To Joshua, Gideon, Gabriel, Logan, and Adam Joseph, my future missionary sons, and all others of your "royal generation." Your father has written this for you because "if ye are prepared . . . ye shall not fear." (D&C 38:30.)

Picture used by permission.

CONTENTS

Preface 1
I **THE ROYAL GENERATION**
    One   You Are Hereby Called To Serve 7
    Two   I Hope They Call Me on a Mission 11
    Three   Three Case Studies 19
    Four   Foreordination and the Royal Generation 31
    Five   Sister Missionaries 43
II **GETTING READY**
    Six   If Ye Are Prepared 55
    Seven   Getting Ready: A Practical Guide 63
    Eight   The Successful Missionary 71
    Nine   I'll Go Where You Want Me to Go 83
    Ten   Looking Forward To the MTC 91
III **PARENTS AND GIRLS WHO WAIT**
    Eleven   Will She Wait? 99
    Twelve   A Matter of Faith 111
    Thirteen   Dear John 119
    Fourteen   Mom and Dad 127
Epilogue 137

PREFACE

For some years now it has been my happy assignment to share with Latter-day Saint youth the joy that comes from missionary service and the importance of sincere preparation for that service. I am often asked, "Where can we obtain a copy of this material?" "Are these concepts written down anywhere? They're so logical. They need to be written down somewhere for reference." This book is a response to those questions.

Missionaries, Parents, and Girls Who Wait is directed especially toward those who will someday serve missions, particularly those young men who now hold the Aaronic Priesthood. It will also be an assistance to those missionaries now serving in the field who feel in their hearts that there must be a way they can do even better. It will also prove quite informative (and even, we have found, surprising) to all those who are interested in those young men, such as mothers and fathers, bishops and advisers, and, of course, girl friends.

To avoid the awkward repetition of "him or her" and "he or she," I have generally referred to the prospective missionary in the masculine gender (men comprise ninety-three percent of the missionary force throughout the world today). However, the information contained herein applies equally to young women who are considering missions.

I feel impressed to share with the reader the fact that I have often felt the guiding hand of the Lord as I have tried to work on this endeavor in a manner that would be pleasing to Him. It is to that Spirit which enlightens us all that I publicly and reverently offer my deepest and most sincere appreciation.

In addition, there have been numerous others who have had a great deal to do with what you're about to read. These great "torch bearers," as I see them, have kindly and graciously shared the light of their knowledge and understanding that we might all be lifted.

Although space does not allow mentioning all those involved, I feel the need to identify and offer my deepest appreciation to at least a few. Their inclusion is not intended to imply, directly or indirectly, their endorsement of this work, or to relieve the author of full responsibility for its content.

I deeply express my gratitude and heartfelt thanks to certain General Authorities of the Church of Jesus Christ of Latter-day Saints: President Spencer W. Kimball; Elders J. Thomas Fyans, A. Theodore Tuttle, William R. Bradford, and Paul H. Dunn of the First Quorum of Seventy. To the members of the Church Missionary Committee, especially Robert L. Swensen, Director of Pre-Mission Services; to Dr. Henry B. Eyring, Church Commissioner of Education, whose love and respect for our youth sets such a fine example for us all; to numerous administrators and faculty at Brigham Young University who were so kind and generous with their time and suggestions, particularly Dr. Jeffrey R. Holland, President; Dr. Robert J. Matthews, Dean of the Department of Religion; and Dr. Truman G. Madsen, Coordinator of Judeo-Christian Studies of the Religious Studies Center; to the administrators and staff at the Missionary Training Center who serve the missionary cause so well, most especially Dr. Joe J. Christensen, President, and Bishop Allen C. Ostergar, Administrative Director of Training; to my good friend and colleague, Dr. Paul

R. Warner, Director of B.Y.U. Pre-Service for Seminaries and Institutes; to a legion of enthused and responsive mission presidents such as Kenneth W. Godfrey, former president of the Pennsylvania Pittsburgh Mission, F. Wayne Chamberlain, former president of the Canada Calgary Mission, and numerous other mission presidents, missionaries, and friends mentioned within these pages.

Lastly, my heartfelt appreciation to my sweetheart and companion, Lynne, who not only served as a sounding board and so willingly offered counsel and suggestions, but also patiently and repeatedly cleared out the kids and diverted the phone calls so that Dad could concentrate on the task at hand.

Part I

The Royal Generation

1
YOU ARE HEREBY CALLED TO SERVE

Certain events in life are never forgotten: falling in love for the first time; being in an embarrassing roadshow; setting a school record; gazing upon your newborn child; and what you were doing when *your* mission call arrived. Ask any missionary what he or she was doing when the mailman made that fateful delivery, and the initial response always seems to be a smile.

Have you ever wondered about that moment? It's scary, thrilling, intriguing, exciting, overwhelming, and very, very humbling. It opens a new chapter of your life.

It is therefore quite apropos to open the first chapter of this book with The *Call*. I pray each of you young men (and many of you young sisters) who read these pages will live worthy to receive this kind of letter someday with *your* name and address on it, signed by the prophet of the living God.

Please read the call slowly—reverently. And begin to understand the incredible eternal implications contained therein.

THE CHURCH OF JESUS CHRIST OF LATTER-DAY SAINTS
Office of the First Presidency
47 East South Temple Street, Salt Lake City, Utah 84150

July 22, 1982

Elder Todd Bartley Smith
Bountiful 46th,
Bountiful Utah Mueller Park
2161 South 1150 East
Bountiful, Utah 84010

Dear Elder Smith:

You are hereby called to serve as a missionary of The Church of Jesus Christ of Latter-day Saints to labor in the Chile Vina Del Mar Mission for a period of 18 months.

You should report to the Missionary Training Center in Provo, Utah on Thursday, October 21, 1982.

You have been recommended as one worthy to represent the Lord as a minister of the restored gospel. You will be an official representative of the Church. As such, you will be expected to maintain highest standards of conduct and appearance by keeping the commandments, living mission rules, and following the counsel of your mission president.

You will also be expected to devote all your time and attention to serving the Lord, leaving behind all other personal affairs. As you do these things, the Lord will bless you and you will become an effective advocate and messenger of the Truth. We place in you our confidence and pray that the Lord will help you meet your responsibilities.

The Lord will reward the goodness of your life. Greater blessings and more happiness than you have yet experienced await you as you humbly and prayerfully serve the Lord in this labor of love among his children.

We ask that you please send your written acceptance promptly, endorsed by your bishop.

Sincerely,

[signature]
President

2
I HOPE THEY CALL ME ON A MISSION

"I hope they call me on a mission
When I have grown a foot or two.
I hope by then I will be ready
To teach and preach and work as missionaries do."
—Sing with Me, B-75

I remember the day all too well. It was a typical "last week in school" at Bountiful (Utah) High School Seminary. Practical jokes were becoming epidemic. Not only that, the word was out that Brother Carver (who taught one of the sophomore classes down the hall) was organizing his students to toilet paper my car again. It was turning out to be one of those days. Walking into the shelter of my office (it seemed a safer place, somehow), I became aware of two junior boys mumbling in the hallway. They were just leaving their seminary class where a lesson had evidently been given on the importance of preparing for a mission. They were feeling a little cocky about it.

"Do you think you're gonna go?"

"Oh, I dunno," replied the other. "Maybe if there are no more good lookin' girls left," he continued, as they both had a good laugh.

Well that did it! Now it was my turn. As a joke I burst through the door, grabbed the bigger boy by his lapels, and pinned him against the wall. "What'd you say?" I demanded, sneering and trying as hard as I could to look stern.

They were pretty sure I was joking (I was), but then again—maybe I wasn't.

"Uh, w-w-we were j-j-just talking about g-g-going on our missions," gasped the taller of the two. He had to gasp because of my grip on the neck of his jacket.

"If there are no good looking girls left—is that what you said? Well, let me ask you something, Chuckles—" (His name was Chuck; he knew who I was and that I tend to tease my students a lot, but right now he thought it best to listen attentively, just in case. Smart boy. I was just getting warmed up.)

"What do you think would happen to this Church," I continued, "if the magnificent Charles _____ decided not to go on a mission? Do you think it would crumble and fall apart or something?"

"Well, n-n-no . . . I didn't mean that," he stammered.

"You better believe it wouldn't, Charlie! So the point isn't whether you're going to do the Church any great favors by going on a mission or not—the point is, are you able to get your act together and become worthy so that you can hope and pray that someday the prophet might see fit to allow you to have one of the greatest opportunities of a lifetime. Right?"

"Y-y-y-yes s-s-sir," he squeaked.

Still holding him up on his tiptoes by the front of his jacket, I glanced over at his companion who had slowly backed away toward the exit at the end of the hall.

Realizing I was now eyeing him, he stopped abruptly. Searching for the proper words, he finally blurted, "Right! Oh, *right!*"

Satisfied, I slowly released my grip and smoothed out the ruffled lapel. "Fine, men, we'll have to have another little chat again sometime. It's nice to see how much you've matured in the last few minutes." I allowed a grin to spread across my face. Then we all had a nice laugh together.

The following school year they recalled the incident. "We really didn't know if you were joking or not, Brother Mickel!" Although I was, the point I felt I wanted to make was something I never kid about. You see, this big, wonderful Church of ours will go right on growing and progressing whether we decide to serve missions to our fellow man or not. So too often some of us might have the mistaken notion that we're doing the Church a big "favor" by going on a mission. But think—who *really* gets the most out of your mission? *You* do!

Anyway, they both got the point. Have you? Oh, I know there will be those you will reach, and perhaps convert, whose families will call your name blessed throughout all eternity, but still, *you* are the one who benefits most from your mission! Returned missionaries often admit that while one of the factors that originally motivated them involved the desire for personal growth, they nonetheless learned that true greatness really comes from effectively learning to lose ourselves in the service of others. (Mosiah 2:17.) Isn't our prophet a great example of that?

What may be less obvious is that the same lesson holds true in building a successful marriage. Do you see any advantage to the husband who has already learned that lesson because he fulfilled a successful mission? Oh, the rewards that can come from the simple principles of obedience! And not because we *have* to, but because we *want* to.

Walk down a line of high school graduates and ask, "What are you going to be?"

"I want to be an astronaut," or "I want to be an attorney," or "I want to be an Avon lady."

"I want to pump gas" or "I want to be a minister."

"Minister?"

"Yes."

Is that person sincere? Absolutely. Times have changed from the way it was when the Savior walked the earth. Now some of us Christians think we can tell the Lord we are going to be His ministers. It wasn't always that way.

Look in the fifteenth chapter of John. How did the Savior do it when He was here? He was ready to begin His ministry. How long did he prepare for His mission? Thirty years. How long have you brethren been preparing?

Now the Savior starts calling individuals to positions in His Church. Think about this for a minute now. Among the first that He called was Andrew and his brother Simon who later became known as Peter. He calls out to them, "Drop your nets, and come follow me."

These were some pretty tough fellows. They were involved in one of the more "macho" jobs of their day. They were fishermen. They worked out in the sun all day long heaving those huge nets out as far as they could throw them. They were dirty, grimy, sweaty, hard-working men.

Picture yourself out in that boat, working in the hot sun with your calloused hands and gritty determination. And here comes this fellow standing on the shore, and he's saying, "Come follow me, and I will make you fishers of men." What would be your "natural man" response? How would you react?

Well, what did they do? Mark says "straightway they forsook their nets, and followed him." (Mark 1:18.)

How were they listening to Him? They heard with their *spiritual* ears, not the way most folks listen. The sensation they felt seemed to say, "I *know* that blessed voice. There's something very special about what He's just said, and *I'm going to follow that man!*" So they dropped their nets and followed Him.

When He got all twelve of them together, He did something very significant. He laid his hands upon their heads individually, and He said, "You have not chosen me." Did you catch that? "*You have not chosen me,* but *I have chosen you,* and ordained you, that ye should go and bring forth fruit." (John 15:16. Italics added.)

This brings us back to our fine, sincere young high school graduate who says, "I'm going to be His minister." But who, honestly, is doing the choosing in that case?

One of the arrows below represents nearly all Christian churches today. The other represents our church. Do you know which is which?

Not too long ago the leaders of one of the largest of the Christian churches met together to decide who their new leader was going to be. When that situation arose in Christ's time, we learn from the scriptures that the leaders made their decisions based on the principle or "rock" of revelation. But most churches don't do it that way anymore. As a matter of fact, they can't because most of them have mandated that the heavens are closed, and therefore there is no more revelation.

So, as has become the pattern of most Christian churches today, these leaders came to a decision by simply voting. History has demonstrated that when voting occurs, it is generally preceded by varying degrees of campaigning, politicking, and even compromise. Now compromise may be the way to go in politics and other systems organized by the ingenuity of man, but when you attempt to compromise truth, truth begins to die, for truth compromised is no longer truth.

And so it is that decisions for what used to be a divine church are no longer the result of revelation from God to man, but rather man trying to instruct God. In other words, the arrow no longer points down (from the heavens to the earth); now it points up (man telling God).

Can you imagine children "voting" on whether their father had the capacity to speak, and later, whether he even had a physical body or not? How would you feel if someday someone voted that you no longer had a body? Would that stop your body from existing? Of course not, but that's the kind of nonsense our Heavenly Father witnessed when a group of His children got together in A.D. 325 and "voted" away His body.

After the "vote" was taken nobody at the meeting could explain it either, much less defend it scripturally, so it was decided to do away with the need to understand it by proclaiming it a "mystery." It became so hard to understand that the doctrine was called by its earthly creators the "great incomprehensible mystery."

Now we know that our Father in Heaven is really our father and wants us to call Him that (Matthew 6:9); that He is *real*, that He *cares*, that He is a God of passions (Exodus 4:14); that He wants us to draw close to Him (D&C 88:63). We know that He even commands that we try to become like Him (John 17:3) so that He might share His happiness with His children (Romans 8:7). Indeed the arrow still comes down, or at least it does in *His* church.

However, Satan has had his way for a long time, and he's not going to give it up without a fight. The greatest darkness that has come upon this world in a long time is here now. It hovers over this earth and controls most of the world. Lucifer is having a great time.

And into this thick darkness go a few young ones with torches in their hands to pierce and hurt the evil darkness. We call them missionaries. They rely on that arrow coming down to give them inspiration and revelation to confound the so-called "learned" men of this generation with the simple saving truths of the gospel. (Isaiah 29:14.)

Can you see how ineffective and even helpless we would be without that arrow? We would be just another sect teaching people to live a good life. But *with* that arrow, we are the kingdom of God on earth. How wonderful it is to be a part of such a marvelous plan!

Some Interesting References

1. On reading the Bible with the pages "open" as contrasted with reading it "closed": *Matthew Cowley Speaks* (Salt Lake City: Deseret Book Company, 1954), pp. 85-87.
2. Check your local library for any number of sources that discuss the Nicean Council.
3. "The Existence and Duration of the Spirit," by Orson Pratt in *Temples of the Most High,* N. B. Lundwall (Salt Lake City: Bookcraft, 1962), pp. 291-93.

3
THREE CASE STUDIES

1. Danny the Sophomore

I was surprised to see him. His lanky, athletic frame pretty well filled the doorway of my office.

I knew him mostly by reputation: All-State wrestler, fast with the girls, enjoyed getting bombed on weekends, fought with his father (who was in the bishopric) almost constantly. He was cocky and unusually sure of himself, yet as he stood there he looked mostly nervous and anything but cocky.

He was hurting inside, and he didn't know why. The emotional pain was ripping him apart. So he was taking the ultimate step—lowering himself (it's so hard to do when you're "cool") to the point of actually talking it over with an (ugh) seminary teacher.

At my invitation he entered, commandeered a nearby chair, and began to unload. He didn't want to talk about his lifestyle, but instead he wanted to share with me the feelings of agitation, frustration, and remorse he was experiencing. "I keep trying to act *cool*," he finally confided, "but something is starting to rip me apart on the inside. Somehow, I kept thinking you'd know what it was. And if you promise not to lecture me like my dad always does, I'd like you to tell me why I'm feeling this way."

Immediately sensing a great opportunity to be of service to my fellow man and seizing upon it, I dug deep into my wells of wisdom and reservoirs of profound knowledge, looked at him solemnly for several moments to set the proper mood, and then in a voice so low and calm that he had to lean forward to hear it, I shook my head and said, "I'm afraid I don't know, Danny."

"What'd you say?"

"I said I don't know."

"What'dya mean, you don't know!"

"I don't have your answer," I shrugged.

He looked defeated.

"Would you like to ask someone who does?"

"Like who?" he inquired, beginning to have hope again.

I slipped onto my knees. "Come on," I invited.

"Oh, I'm not very good at that."

"Do you want answers or don't you? Are you afraid of what you might find out?"

"No. I really want to know."

"Then come on," I persisted. "I'm not gonna ask by myself."

He was still reticent. "Will you do the talking?" He was growing more humble now.

"If that's what you want."

Slowly he came to the floor, and we were on our knees together, two brothers, talking it over with Father.

When it was over, we both stayed on the floor, leaning back against the wall. It seemed more appropriate.

After a while, I spoke. "What did you get, Dan?"

A long pause followed. Then, "He's there, isn't He." It

wasn't a question.

"Yeah, Dan. He's there."

"What does He want me to do?"

"I didn't get it all, Dan. You'll have to fill in the pieces later. But what I got was pretty specific. Can you handle it?"

He thought a moment. Then, "Yeah, I really need to know." No more coolness, no more cockiness. Something real was about to take place.

"You made some commitments before you came here."

"No, I didn't."

"I mean in the first estate. You know, your preexistence?"

"Oh."

"That's right, Danny. Apparently, you were someone pretty special there, a very noble spirit, I'd say. Doesn't your patriarchal blessing tell you something about that?"

"I sorta never got around to getting one. . ."

"Oh, I see. Well, looks as though it's time to come up with a revised priority list, my friend. Some people are getting burned because of you."

"Who? What people?" A few pieces were starting to fall into place now.

"Evidently, people you promised to bring the gospel to. Remember those commitments in the preexistence we were talking about?"

"Yes."

"Well, they agreed to be born in places where it's hard to find out about the gospel. Because you were their friend you promised to bring it to them when we all got down here on earth."

"So what does that mean?"

"Well, they don't know now (because of the veil of forgetfulness) that it's the gospel they're missing, but they know they're missing something. And in their own way, they're making their frustrations known, and the Lord's just taking all those frustrations he's hearing from them and dumping them, so to speak, right in your lap, which is right where they belong."

"And that's causing the bad feelings I've been getting." He paused. "Is that how it always works?"

"No, I don't think so. You're one of the lucky ones. You're feeling so much guilt that you want to do something about it."

"How long do you think I have?" He was nearing the end of his sophomore year.

"It's not the same for everybody. The smart ones don't take on the problems in the first place. I think you're feeling it so strong now because for you, it's almost too late."

He took a long pause, rubbed his eyes, and sighed. Then he looked up past the ceiling, and sighed again.

* * * * * * * * * *

From that day on he began to change. He was too sharp not to. He couldn't go at nineteen as his friends did. For him it was almost too late to start changing even as a sophomore. But he did go. My, how he did go!

There are a lot of "Dannys" out there. Some have already written themselves off. The Lord hasn't. This chapter is for them. And their girl friends. And their parents. And the families whose lives they will have an eternal effect upon when they enter the mission field.

For them especially Elder William R. Bradford makes this choice comment:

> For those of you who feel you cannot serve because you have slipped into transgression I would say, don't

despair. There is a way back. The plan of repentance really works. You can take steps to return to full worthiness. You can make acceptable restitution and place yourself in the service of the Lord.

. . . You must prepare. You must now make yourselves worthy and available. If you do not, the work will go on without you. It will go on at a slower pace, but it will go on. If you are not part of it, if you do not do your duty, what will happen to you? How will you be sanctified? (*Ensign*, November 1981, pp. 50-51.)

You can do it, my brothers! Danny did. You read his case study. Perhaps you'd like to read one or two more.

2. Bruce Martin

I've never met Bruce Martin, but he sent me the following story with instructions to use it or any portion of it as I saw fit.

> I began becoming inactive as a result of staying out late on Saturday nights. Soon however, I was not only missing priesthood meeting but Sunday School and sacrament meetings as well. It seemed every Sunday I had a reason why I couldn't go to church.
>
> In order to become "popular" I began to sacrifice my church standards for my friends' approval. I wanted to be "free" from the standards of the Church and do what everyone else was doing. The Word of Wisdom was the first to go and soon I was smoking and drinking. I was doing whatever was necessary to become "popular."
>
> It was during this troublesome time in my life that I developed a negative attitude toward the Church and its teachings. My parents became deeply

concerned about what I was doing to my life. They tried to express their love and concern by counseling me to uphold the standards they had taught me.

In doing so they made me feel guilty and uncomfortable. To counter those feelings I became very rebellious and withdrew further and further from the Church. I was obtaining what I thought was "freedom."

The preceding spring I had decided to attend BYU and had applied and been accepted for the following fall semester. However, during the final weeks before I was to leave for BYU, my nonmember friends began applying pressure for me not to go. So convincing were they that I did decide not to go and to attend a different institution.

My last step was to inform my parents of my decision and let them know that I did not intend to go to BYU. My father, being inspired of the Lord, talked with me for over an hour about what I should do and his feelings about my decision. While talking with him the Holy Ghost touched my spirit and I knew what I must do.

So, after two years of inactivity, I traveled to Provo with my parents. My family wanted to attend Education Week so we arrived about ten days before the fall semester was to start. As far as I knew I didn't have a testimony, and I still didn't care about getting one.

I refused to attend Education Week for the first couple of days, but then, because there was nothing better to do, I decided to attend a couple of the youth-oriented classes.

In those classes I felt the spiritual conversation I needed to motivate me to repentance. Even though I had attended church most of my life and had been raised by tremendous parents, I had, as yet, not asked the Lord what I should do. I had not sincerely searched to know the truth.

I attended the series taught by David R. Mickel. After the first day I was troubled. The Holy Ghost had touched my spirit and I knew that I needed more than I currently had. Then during the course of the next couple of days, I learned what it was that I was lacking.

I wanted to be free! I wanted to be free from the sins that I was caught up in. Before, I wanted to be free from the restraints that the Lord had placed upon his children, but now I wanted the spiritual freedom that comes from obeying the commandments.

After the class I got on my motorcycle and rode and rode. Finally I stopped and rested. Out of habit I pulled out a cigarette and lit it up but as soon as I did, I was overwhelmed by feelings of guilt. I grabbed the cigarette, threw it on the ground, and crushed it. Then I took what was left of the pack and threw it as far as I could. At that moment, I resolved to turn my life around and start living the commandments.

I realized that real freedom comes not by disobeying the commandments but by obeying them. I realized that by living within the framework that God has set up I could be free from sin and the feelings of guilt that accompany sin. That was what I wanted. That was what I needed.

I am currently serving a mission for The Church of Jesus Christ of Latter-day Saints and laboring to bring others to this spiritual conviction. I know that if I live worthily that I can bear witness, with the power of the Holy Ghost, that God lives, that Jesus is the Christ and that if we will obey the commandments, we will find happiness.

Of course, my classes weren't what made such important changes in Bruce Martin's life. He was a young person who saw the *need* for a change, and then took the steps necessary to bring about that change. He placed himself in an environment where the Spirit of the Lord could work its wonderful effects upon him.

3. Douglas Thatcher

When I heard that Doug had been appointed assistant to the mission president in the Philippines, I had to chuckle as I recalled the hassle he and I caused each other a few years earlier when I was his seminary teacher during his senior year in high school. After we became friends, he came by my office three different times to say goodbye. Each time he had been kicked out of school and was leaving to join the Army. Each time something happened that changed his course. I thought you'd like to read his story, too.

> It all started in junior high when I began to run around with friends who did not have the same standards that my parents had taught me. The things that they were doing were all so new to me that it was not long before I began to do the same things. They were not members of the Church and instead of helping them into the Church and to realize what they were doing was wrong, I found it easier to conform to what they were doing. I developed a bad attitude toward my parents and what they were trying to do for me. I began to pull away from them.
>
> High school came and I found myself in my senior year still with this attitude and thinking that I needed to show everyone that I was cool and tough. It's easy to look back now and say how foolish the things that I was doing were, but I remember how

important they seemed at the time. At seventeen I thought to be cool you had to drink beer and let everyone know that you were tough. Many times this attitude got me into trouble. I built up a bad reputation in school and did not know if I wanted to finish school or even if I would be allowed to stay in school even if I wanted to because of my poor attendance and lousy attitude. I thought about joining the Army and getting away from it all. I had no intention of facing up to the problems in my life, and it seemed easier just to get away.

I began thinking of joining the Army. Then I talked to a seminary teacher who fortunately took the time to help me think through some things. We talked about a lot of ideas that I had been through with many teachers before, and it began to sound like an old song. But this time there was a new thought, something that I had never thought about before. What would the future have in store for me if I kept on acting as I was? How could I eventually get married and expect to teach my sons how to become men if I hadn't become one myself? What would they learn about important things like "commitment" if I couldn't teach them by my own example? He challenged me to start doing those things that would really make a *man* out of me, and to stop playing little-boy games. This thought really impressed me, and it caught me off guard so I had to think about it. I knew this was important because in my whole life I never doubted that the Church was true, and I had always gone to my meetings. I guess that that is where I got the idea that I would someday "straighten up" and get my life in order. The problem was that I was always waiting for next week or next month to take the steps. I learned that with an attitude like I had in life, and had I not finally realized that I needed to do it "now" I suppose that I would be in the situation that a lot of my old friends are in now. They are, for the most part, still getting into trouble and doing things to themselves that will lead them nowhere. Looking at them gives me a good idea where I would have been had I not changed.

I realized that I needed to change, but the road was not easy. First I stopped running around with my old crowd and found some great friends who would help me rather than lead me nowhere. I really got into seminary and the lessons taught there. At last I was doing what I should, and it felt great. The desire to get my life in order brought me many good experiences, and I see now that the hand of the Lord guided me into them. I began to progress and to realize my potential.

During this time of change this teacher said that going on a mission was one of the things that would "make a man out of me." I hated it when he used those words, because I knew he really had me pegged and that he was right about me. So I set my mind on a mission, and when the call came to go to the Asian people and teach them the gospel, I accepted it. The mission field brought me to a true knowledge of myself and what I could do. A lot of the things that meant so much to me before really didn't mean so much any more. I discovered that it is cool to be spiritual and that if you are a man, you don't need to prove it to anyone, people just know.

After nineteen years of doing nothing but taking from people, I got the chance to give to others, and it felt great. I know that repentance works and that you can put the past behind you if you want to. I'm looking forward now to the day when I can sit down with my future sons and feel strong when I talk to them about words like "commitment" and self-respect, and what it feels like to become a man.

It was Paul who taught us, "When I was a child, I spake as a child, I understood as a child, I thought as a child: but when I became a man, I put away childish things." (1 Corinthians 13:11.)

Through these three great examples I'm sure many others will make that great decision to finally, once and for all, put away childish things. I know I had to make that decision myself. Thank you for your great examples, my brothers.

Now learn how to get ready to go!

We're about to, but first, let's find out just exactly who we really are.

4
FOREORDINATION AND THE ROYAL GENERATION

In teaching youth there is one thought that guides much of my thinking. I absolutely refuse to treat you as anything less than what inspired prophets have designated you to be—the Royal Generation. I'm tired of seeing you pampered or pandered to. I think that's an insult to who you are. It's your destiny to become great—if you're willing to pay the price for achieving that greatness.

There's never been a generation like this before—an entire generation of princes who made commitments while in their first estate that they would serve missions in their second estate. In my generation that was not true.

Three months before I turned nineteen I went home for Christmas vacation from college. My bishop saw me at church and pulled me over to a corner of the foyer. "David, are you getting ready for your mission?"

"Yes, sir, I'm looking forward to it."

"Fine, we'll make plans for this summer, okay?"

And eight months later I received my call from President David O. McKay to go to Uruguay.

One of my roommates at school was also from California. When he went home for vacation his bishop asked him about his plans for a mission.

"Oh, I don't think so—I've met this really neat girl," he answered.

"Oh, I see. Well, okay then," his bishop said.

And that was it; no pressure. And so he didn't go.

My roommate went on to marry that sweet girl and years later was called to be a bishop himself. I've heard this fine man tell the members of his ward that he would have given *anything* if his bishop had pushed him just a little more to go on a mission. But that wasn't his bishop's fault because in those days the bishop had not been told to do so, so he didn't. It was an optional way of serving the Lord then.

But that's not the case anymore. For the first time since the Lord initiated missionary work in His church, He has instructed His prophet that *this* is the generation, this is the royal priesthood that has been saved up until this glorious time. *This* is the vanguard generation leading to the final battle. That may be why, brethren, so many of you are feeling "antsy" and anxious about the day that call comes from a living prophet. That also may be why some of you are feeling uncomfortable and nervous if you even consider some excuse that would keep you from going. To do so would be contrary to what you committed to do long, long ago.

When President Jeffrey R. Holland served as a Stake High Councilor, he gave a talk in our ward in Bountiful, Utah, in 1978, and spoke specifically to the teenage brethren:

> Everything I read in scripture about our premortal experience indicates the intensity of the struggle there between those—especially Christ—who supported our Father's plan and those who

followed Lucifer in his opposition to it. We chose to fight for righteousness then, and I don't see how we can do less now. Who can withhold himself—from a full-time mission or any other necessary service in the work of exaltation? To do so would be to deny our premortal commitments and the declarations we made there in keeping our first estate.

What does our prophet have to say? In an address to seminary and institute personnel in 1975, President Kimball stated that:

> A mission is not a casual thing—it is not an alternative program of the Church. Neither is a mission a matter of choice any more than tithing is a choice, any more than the Word of Wisdom is a choice . . . . Every normal young man is as much obligated to go on a mission as he is to pay his tithing, attend his meetings, keep the Sabbath day holy, and keep his life spotless and clean. Can you accept that?

He's talking to you brethren definitely, and many of you sisters, too. You of the chosen generation. You of the royal priesthood! And if you're feeling stirrings that you haven't felt before or perhaps for a very long time, those are eternal chords being strummed deep within you. There are sons and daughters of God out there, your spiritual brothers and sisters, waiting for you to respond, and sacrifice, and bring them the gospel light! We pleaded for this opportunity before we came, and now it's here.

Years ago in a missionary conference presided over by Elder J. Thomas Fyans we were instructed with the following words that startled some of us there:

> I believe that you have been picked to come here to this (Uruguayan) mission and reserved until these latter days because before this life you had very close contact with some eternal spirits who are now

waiting for you here (in Uruguay). And when you find these people, your hearts will reach out and find each other, and the Spirit of the Holy Ghost will encircle you and lock together your reunion with that Spirit.

I remember my anxiety to go out and find those people and experience that special spiritual reunion promised by President Fyans. And I did! Meeting them has changed my life forever. I promise it will change yours, too, as soon as you decide to let it.

Interestingly, one of my own seminary students, Elder Bryce Thacker, found that promise fulfilled quite literally while on his mission to Scotland. During the confirmation prayer for one of his converts the branch president was inspired to tell the convert that the elders who had taught him had promised to do so in the preexistence. Can you imagine the deeply reflective feelings Bryce and his companion experienced after hearing that?

The gospel has a familiar sound to many who join the Church. Missionaries are called specifically to seek out those with what is sometimes referred to as "believing blood." Dr. Truman G. Madsen reports that "The Prophet said that one day we will discover that all of us, regardless of our present guesses and researchings . . . will find that there is in our veins the cumulative blood of Israel. . . . It is intended by the Almighty that we belong literally to the family of Abraham and those of us who have mostly "Gentile" inheritance will find that through the renovating powers of the Holy Ghost we are made as Joseph said, literally of the blood of Abraham by a process called the sanctification of the Holy Ghost." It is interesting to note also that the Prophet Joseph Smith had a vision through the Urim and Thummim in which he saw that only five generations previously he shared a common ancestor with Orson and Parley Pratt, Brigham Young, Newell K. Whitney, Orson Hyde, Wilford Woodruff, and others. Out of one common ancestor, one John Lathrop, came a veritable "Who's Who" of first generation Mormons!

As Dr. Robert J. Matthews points out, "We cannot read the scriptures very far without encountering the word *covenant* . . . . The ancient patriarchs . . . sought assurance from the Lord that the same gospel would come to their posterity. In response the Lord promised to offer the gospel to their children in future generations." (*Ensign*, December 1980, pp. 33-39.)

Speaking to high school students, Dr. Henry B. Eyring used the following story to support that thrilling concept that there are many who respond to the gospel because it strikes a familiar chord within them:

> It was August 24, 1939. Germany was going to war and the borders would soon be closed. The mission president in Frankfurt was deeply troubled. Somewhere between Frankfurt and the Dutch border thirty-one missionaries were unaccounted for. He felt impressed to send an elder to find them. The elder was a former football player, over two hundred pounds, but that would scarcely help him in this assignment. Thousands of people crowded trains and train stations in panic. Those thirty-one missionaries could be anywhere in the trains, stations, or cities. The president gave the young elder 500 marks, tickets to Denmark and London for the thirty-one elders and sent him on his errand.
>
> The elder took the train to Cologne where he felt an impression to get off. He got off. The huge station was jammed with people, many young travelers, many looking like the missionaries the elder must find. He had no idea in what place or even in what city to look. To find anyone would have been impossible. He began to whistle their missionary song, "Do What Is Right." Three missionaries came out of the crowd.

The big elder gave them money and tickets and boarded another train headed toward Holland. Whenever he felt impressed in a town or village, he got off. He gave the whistle. And missionaries came to the familiar sound. Finally, all thirty-one missionaries reached safety.

Perhaps a score of my contacts who joined the Church when I was a missionary told me what they had felt in their hearts when they accepted the gospel. Not one said that I had convinced them or even that I had changed their minds. In a variety of phrasings, each said essentially, "I recognized what you taught me. What you taught me was what I always thought to be true."

They seemed to have known the sound of truth. And they knew it before I taught it to them, although perhaps vaguely. They recognized the sound, as did those missionaries long ago in Germany. And they came to it.

You have the blessing of the seed of Abraham. You have the most precious thing on earth, the gospel of Jesus Christ. And you have the obligation of the seed of Abraham. That's why you may not have been surprised to hear a prophet of God say that every healthy young priesthood holder has the obligation to prepare himself to serve a worthy mission. If you listened, in your heart, you knew that was true. I'm not sure whether that is because we have a trace of memory left from interviews long ago, in the preexistence, or because the Holy Ghost has taught us here. But if you are very quiet, so that you can hear the small voice, that command of a prophet will have a familiar sound.

Don't feel badly if you haven't recognized that sound yet. The elder who went looking in the station in Cologne had heard only the voice of the Spirit to get off the train. But it took more than the voice of the Spirit to get the three missionaries to him. It took his whistling to call them. Others might not have even recognized the whistled tune and known it was a call. There are degrees of spiritual sensitivity. You can repent, pray, and study the scriptures to increase yours. And when you do, you will recognize in you a desire to give to others the gift you have, the gospel.

Remember the promise to Abraham when you are in missionary service. The scriptures tell us that the seed of Abraham are scattered in every nation. "Scattered" means you will have to look for them, among the crowds. You will have to approach thousands of people and teach hundreds. But I testify that among them, perhaps only when you have endured, you will find those who say, "Oh, yes, I always believed that was true." They will hear the familiar sound because you heard it and responded, as you may have promised you would long ago.

When we combine that familiar sound with the more sure word of prophecy, we possess the embryo of the greatest power source ever known to man. Perhaps the following scriptures may be just a little more significant to you now.

> To this end was I born, and for this cause came I into the world, that I should bear witness of the truth. Everyone that is of the truth heareth my voice. (John 18:37.)
>
> He that entereth in by the door is the shepherd of the sheep. To him the porter openeth; and the sheep hear his voice: and he calleth his own sheep by name, and leadeth them out.
>
> And when he putteth forth his own sheep, he goeth before them, and the sheep follow him: for

they know his voice.

And a stranger they will not follow, but will flee from him: for they know not the voice of strangers. (John 10:1-5.)

It's a glorious time to be a part of this great process and seeing the great plan unfold. It's a glorious time to be who we are, to know exactly where we came from, and to be doing exactly what we should be doing.

When you really think about it, why wouldn't anyone want to serve a mission? Why wouldn't anyone want to prepare for and experience the one adventure that would lay the best foundation for their own happiness, both in this life and ultimately throughout all the eternities with their families?

Can you imagine anything else you could possibly do during those eighteen months that could come anywhere near doing what your mission will do for you? This is a big part of what being a member of the royal generation is all about!

Elder William R. Bradford said during a general conference talk:

> There is concern as to whether all of those who should and could participate in this (missionary) work really understand and believe the basic principles and purposes for which God's decree, to declare this gospel to all the world, was given. Although there are thirty thousand missionaries now serving, there should and could be many times that many.
>
> . . . Some of you say in your minds, "Oh well, you just don't understand my case. My situation is different. I plan to be a great lawyer, or doctor, or athlete, or some other great person.
>
> "Surely neither you nor the Lord would expect me to leave my studies at such an important time. A mission would interfere with my future plans."
>
> Others are thinking, "Yes, I know about mis-

sions, but if you had a girl friend like mine, you'd never leave her. What will happen to her while I'm gone?"

Yet others of you are thinking, "Missions cost so much. I just got this job. I just purchased a car and a stereo. It's just the time of life when I'm starting to get things together for myself. I can't drop all that now. I just can't afford it." . . .

If I could listen to you separately, each case would unfold with one thing in common: all would justify yourselves in not doing your duty to God.

. . . Do you really believe that earthly fame and title, tied to earthly positions and occupations, can compare with God's promises to the faithful? He has promised "thrones, kingdoms, principalities, and powers." He has promised "exaltation and glory in all things." . . . He has promised eternal life. (D&C 132:19.)

I would say to you that you are left without excuse and without justification and that you have placed your eternal salvation in grave danger. William R. Bradford, Oct. 4, 1981 General Conference.)

The director of pre-mission services for the Church, Brother Robert Swensen, directed some remarks to this Royal Generation:

[Young men] are expected to go on a mission. They have already been called to go on a mission in the first estate. A paraplegic or someone born with a mental deficiency may not have that opportunity; he is not *able*. But if you are able, you are expected to go. The fact that you're a football hero, or you've got a swimming scholarship, or a Fulbright scholarship to Harvard—those things do not matter. Being the star football player for a university does not eliminate the requirement, or sacred obligation, to go on a mission —though it remains your choice, nonetheless.

You still have your agency, but you're still supposed to go on a mission. We're all supposed to return to the celestial kingdom. That's why we're here, to work our way back to the celestial kingdom. Some of us aren't going to make it, but that doesn't negate the fact that that's where we're supposed to be.

Compared to anything else, you cannot do better than a mission. I don't care if you have to give up a scholarship—that's only money. I don't care if you have to give up football—that's nothing, that's insignificant compared to eternal values. I don't care if you have to give up schooling and girlfriends because we've been promised that if we do what the Lord wants us to, he's going to bless us.

There's this nice little package of blessings floating around, and there's only one way that you can get those blessings, and that's going on your mission. Now if you decide not to go, you're not a bad person and you will still receive blessings, but it will be a different package of blessings. You can be a good person and not go on your mission, but there's a package of blessings that you cannot have; they will be forever lost to you if you don't go on a mission.

Now my dear young friends. If there's some among you who have been feeling a little wishy-washy and wondering if you should go or not, I *dare* you to take it to your Heavenly Father in prayer. I *challenge* you! I *beg* you. And then you take that answer and read first your Patriarchal Blessing . . . those glorious challenges and promises! Then you turn again to those solemn words of President Kimball (page 33) and re-read them and notice the warmth and serenity and security that will flush that will flush through your inner soul. Isn't it wonderful to have a purpose? A standard? How marvelous to know that we are important, and that the chosen generation has a job to do! It was President Henry D. Moyle who once said, "Put aside every decision of your life until after your mission." Prepare yourself with a working knowledge of the gospel so when *your* torch is passed out, *you* are there to carry it into the world of darkness. Elder Bradford expresses it this way:

> This is a marvelous plan. It is a process of sanctification. When a missionary is placed in a mission environment of order and discipline, where all that is done is in harmony with the spirit, the missionary experiences a great transformation. The heavens open. Powers are showered out. Mysteries are revealed. Habits are improved. Sanctification begins. Through this process the missionary becomes a vessel of light that can shine forth the gospel of Jesus Christ to a world in darkness.

You and I have the privilege of being a part of this great process, of seeing the plan unfold. What a glorious time to be who we are, to know exactly where we came from, and to be doing exactly what we should be doing.

The Royal Generation includes *you!*

5
SISTER MISSIONARIES

I think I've heard them all: Lotsa Makeup, Lost Mandate, Ludicrous Match, Lamentably Missed, Land of Make-believe, Lonely Magpie, and so forth and so on, ad nauseam.

Mention the initials *LM* (Lady Missionaries) to most elders and you get a silent half-smile and a condescending shrug of the shoulders. The stigma of the "if-you-can't-get-married-you-can-always-go-on-a-mission" attitude of years past has been a hard one to shake, perhaps because in the past there was more truth to that stigma than many care to admit.

I must confess that working with lady missionaries on my own mission was not always the kind of happy experience I wanted to write about in my journal. As a presiding elder, much of my time was spent trying to soothe ruffled feathers between elder missionaries and lady missionaries. The latter were often perceived as a nuisance, a millstone around the supervisor's neck.

I wonder why the realization escaped so many that, in all honesty, a number of the elders were also "nuisances," especially those who had not yet caught the vision of why they were on their missions. Why has it been so difficult for so many to realize that while most missionaries are dedicated, sincere, hard-working laborers (both male and female), there are always a few exceptions to the rule. Those exceptions come in both male and female varieties.

I had been called to preside over a branch in the northern part of our mission, near the Brazilian border. Prior to sending me there, my mission president called me in for a conference. He felt that at some future time the branch of Paysandú would be a bulwark to the mission and the center place of a great interior stake. But at the time this sleepy little branch was in a state of blissful lethargy, and needed a total revitalization. He asked me if I had a preference as to which elders should be assigned there with me. I quickly requested some highly-motivated and spiritual missionaries who also happened to be very good basketball players. With that agreed upon, I was excited to be on my way. Forming a solid branch athletic program to attract young, strong future priesthood holders was a strategy I had used quite successfully in the past.

"Before you leave, elder," he concluded, "I want you to know there will also be two lady missionaries there under your supervision."

"With all due respect, sir," I objected, "I would rather not have the lady missionaries assigned there. With all that you want us to accomplish, I really don't want to spend time baby-sitting."

He smiled that special smile. "Now President Mickel," he said, "I believe you should give these sisters a chance. I think you'll find they'll be a great asset to your program."

Now we all knew President J. Thomas Fyans was an inspired man. And I was never one to confute specific direction from a man I so greatly admired. So I departed, determined to achieve our goal but quite apprehensive of the LMs who would, if past experience held true to form, prove to be a burden to us all. I couldn't help thinking to myself, *Why are they here in the field, anyway? Why aren't they home having children?*

Then I met Sister Martha Evelyn Guthrie. She had the smile of a Mona Lisa and the tenacity of a bulldog. I am now a more humble, repentant, and much wiser man. I salute the sister missionaries proudly and with much appreciation. They have great resilience, tenacity, tenderness, and tremendous determination. God bless you, Sweet Sisters. The Church wants you and needs you.

To Marry or to Missionary?

Now that I'm a little wiser, may I offer an observation?

Nancy was a vivacious, happy, and very pretty ninth-grader. Following a fired-up seminary lesson on the importance of missionary work, she ran up to me and gushed, "Oh, Brother Mickel, all I want to do is go on a mission. I don't even want to think about getting married!"

Three years later she was in my twelfth-grade seminary class. I had just shared with the class some very tender personal experiences Sister Mickel and I had enjoyed in raising our children when Nancy approached me excitedly. "Oh, Brother Mickel, I want to have children so bad!"

"You do? But I thought you were planning on a mission?"

She sighed. "Yes, I want that, too. I'm so confused. What should I do?"

I paused for a moment before answering. "Nancy, is there anything you could do to prepare for a mission that wouldn't make you a better mother? Or is there anything you can do to prepare for marriage and parenthood that wouldn't make you a more effective representative of the Lord in the mission field?"

She replied in the negative to both questions.

"Then why not prepare yourself for both, and stay enough in tune with Heavenly Father so that when the time comes for you to receive guidance, you can let *Him* tell you what is best for you at that time in your life?"

She smiled a relieved and happy smile, and felt she had

found the right answer. Since then her sister (and two brothers) have served missions. Nancy herself married a fine young returned missionary in the Los Angeles Temple and is thoroughly enjoying being a brand-new mom to their recently-born son, little Isaac.

May I recommend the same guidance to you girls who are interested in charting your course? Prepare for *both,* and then ask Heavenly Father what He thinks.

Joe J. Christensen, president of the Missionary Training Center, says, "No one loses by preparing to be an excellent missionary whether they are called or not. . . . The experience of a mission helps (a young woman) to be a better mother, wife, and church worker after a mission." President Christensen married an RLM (returned lady missionary) and declares that "that's made a difference in our children's lives and in my life. She brings a tremendous cultural advantage into our home, also."

Karen Christensen (no relation to President Joe Christensen), a RLM who served in Zurich, Switzerland, shares the following insights:

"The basic question asked of every lady missionary is: why did you decide to go? The reasons are as varied or routine as those the elders give, although the choice is usually made independently and the pressures facing the elders are not the same. Perhaps a sister comes from an all-girl family and goes to please her father. Many sisters have completed a college education and do not want to work or continue studies, choosing a mission as a spiritual 'break.' Running away from an uncomfortable social situation is an easy (though very unwise) reason. On the other hand, knowing it is the Lord's will or going out of personal desire gives any missionary a head start. Some of the finest sisters I know fought for years before going, feeling a little reluctant even after the call was extended, but answering the call because they knew it was the Lord's will.

"In my own case, filling a mission was a lifelong goal. Both my parents had filled missions, and I delighted in hearing their experiences as well as those of other relatives. Living in the mission field must have influenced me, too. We had the elders for dinner often, and the more they voiced their opposition to lady missionaries, the more determined I became to go. I guess I wanted to prove that I could go on a mission and still become a wife and mother with plenty of time to spare. But when it came down to the wire, I went because I knew that's where the Lord wanted me. A lot of struggle, prayer, and tears went into that commitment. The stigma of 'old maid' isn't as great now as when I received my call. Many beautiful, talented, intelligent women are accepting—indeed asking—for the call to serve.

"The important thing to remember is not to wait until you think you should go or the Lord desires it, but live your life in accordance with the gospel that you may be prepared for *any* call at *any* time. Develop good study habits; exercise regularly (you may not think a mission is vigorous, but climbing hundreds of stairs a day and riding a bike call for a toned body); eat nutritious meals; be modest and well-groomed; *study* the scriptures; learn to serve others in many different ways; learn how to really pray and rely on the Spirit; develop those aspects of homemaking that will help you develop a foundation for a happy home.

"It's important to develop friendships. Learn how to adjust to differences of opinion, be honest with one another. Develop a sense of humor with yourself and others. I fondly called a companion of mine 'Grace' because she tripped over everything. She replied that she must feel at home because only when she was relaxed was she so clumsy.

"Sister companionships can be very unusual. Pressures cause sisters to be more emotional. If there are differences, they are usually more serious than those between elders.

"Don't be afraid to admit you're wrong. Many a missionary companionship has suffered because of pride; it doesn't need to happen to you, now or then.

"Financial preparation is also a must. Learn that you don't have to get everything you want. Learn to color coordinate and spread your wardrobe out. Be creative with what you have. Work out an agreement with your parents while you're still at home to have your own fixed income for a month in which you completely support yourself, paying rent, utilities, transportation, phone, food, recreation. It will probably be very revealing to you.

"Don't wait until you're called—be a missionary today! Share your testimony. It needn't be in a formal manner, but don't forget to learn to express yourself verbally, too. Invite friends to your home and church activities. Let them see you in action.

"In working with elders, remember that older doesn't always mean right (just what you've been telling your parents for years). In most cases lady missionaries are older and more mature, but they must also learn to respect and follow the priesthood. Be pleasant; patience and love will carry you far and make the elders respect you, too. You'll learn to laugh and cry together.

"During a particularly difficult time early in my missionary training, as I continued studying through a break, one of the elders asked if he could help. I burst into tears of frustration, embarrassment, and gratitude. The next day his companion asked how things were. I was so happy—all had been going very well! I was quite humbled when he asked if I would tell his companion because he had been fasting for me that day.

"What is the advantage of being a lady missionary? Some poorer people are actually put off by the elders' attire. Young men dressed in white shirts, nice suits, knocking on doors of people who can't afford the same sometimes make people feel uncomfortable. Single women are often wary of letting men into their homes, no matter how clean cut they appear to be.

Sisters tend to show emotion more readily. If an investigator is having difficulty, sisters are more likely to be sympathetic, which makes it easier for investigators in certain circumstances to discuss weaknesses.

"Elders and sisters working together complement each other through their strengths and weaknesses. It is often helpful to the elders to have sisters give certain parts of discussions to single women. At times elders who are at a dead end with investigators will ask the sisters to pick up on them, knowing that sometimes a different approach is just what is needed. Sisters are also able to assist in Relief Society, Primary, and Young Women in a special way. Their experience and skills are a great asset in these organizations.

"Sisters are often more attuned to doing the 'little things' to show others how much they care. Sending a note through the mail, making a cake or cookies, taking the time necessary to listen to a troubled soul occur more readily to the sister missionaries. Elders, sometimes afraid of role displacement, often forget the 'little things' that can make such a difference with certain investigator families.

"Serving a mission has been a stepping-stone in my own progression and has opened doors to many experiences I might never have had. Now I more fully understand the principle of love—genuine, unconditional love for brothers and sisters and a yearning that they will understand and accept the gospel of Jesus Christ."

Mission Presidents Speak

Note: A few months ago a number of Mission Presidents responded from their respective Mission Headquarters in different parts of the world to a series of questions I thought you'd like to ask them if you could. They were very anxious to do whatever they could to help you enter the field as prepared as possible. They know you're much more useful to them and to your Heavenly Father that way, and that your own self-confidence, self-respect and self-esteem will increase in accordance with the efforts you make for such preparation. As I will be using their answers to assist you throughout this book, perhaps this would be a good time to introduce them to you. Among those who responded were:

California Oakland Mission ...... Pres. Lindsay R. Curtis
England London Mission .... Pres. Ben E. Lewis
France Paris Mission .... Pres. R. Dean Robinson
New York, New York City Mission
.... Pres. Roland B. Wright
Uruguay Montevideo Mission . Pres. Marion C. Robinson

From now on each time you notice a subsection with the title "MISSION PRESIDENTS SPEAK" in various chapters of this book, you'll know it's time to get ready for a great experience because you'll be hearing counsel right from the experts themselves. This will also be a valuable aid for you missionaries currently in the field if you've been struggling a little or perhaps haven't been having the personal success you think you should be having.[1]

What counsel might you give to our teenage Latter-day Saint girls who are wondering if they should go on a mission?

London: Learn to be spiritually minded and to keep the commandments of the Lord so that she can be worthy to either go on a mission or be married in the temple. Do not go on a mission to "get away" from something or someone. A mission is hard work and not easy. Keep yourself morally clean and avoid engaging in any kind of practice or activity that would rob you of your virtue.

New York: Learn to discipline your life and gain a spiritual testimony of the truth of the gospel. Learn to

---

[1]For a more complete and comprehensive account of the particulars of this study, see *Before The Call*, David R. Mickel; *The New Era*, March 1982, pp. 14-18.

understand the powerful influence that the Holy Ghost can be in your life.

Oakland: Never go on a mission as a means of escape from the possibility that marriage or romance has passed you by. It would be helpful if young girls were required to get their weight down to normal and take a course or two on appearance, makeup, dress, grooming, before they come on missions. Too many are overweight and have emotional problems that should be settled before they enter the mission field.

Montevideo: We are totally in favor of the sister missionaries who come into the mission who are *prepared* and *sincerely dedicated* to the work. Our sister missionaries have contributed immensely to the success of our mission.

Part II
Getting Ready

6
IF YE ARE PREPARED

". . . but if ye are prepared, ye shall not fear."
—D&C 38:30

In 1973 President Kimball gave the following advice in the *New Era:*

> My son, you are heavily obligated for the numerous blessings you enjoy, none of which you have provided yourself, like brains and faculties, sight, hearing. You are the recipient of accumulated "blessings of the ages" and more particularly of the century. Your faith and knowledge of truth are the result of missionary work of days gone by which you can repay by giving to others the same opportunities . . . . Hence it is well for every worthy and prepared young man, as he grows up, to desire mightily to fill a mission. . . . it is incumbent upon each person to prepare himself for that solemn obli-

gation and privilege. (June, pp. 8-9.)

Now that those familiar chords have been strummed within you, and you are beginning to suspect that a mission is right for you, the big question comes up. *How* do I most effectively prepare for a mission? It's really very simple. I am going to lay out before you a sumptuous "smorgasbord" of aids and suggestions. All you have to do is the following:

1. **Pray.** Pray that you will be able to discern how many and which ones of these suggestions pertain to your individual situation.

2. **Read.** Read slowly and carefully. Let each thought sink in. Read not only this chapter, or this section of this book, but be sure to look up President Kimball's article from which the opening quotation was taken: "Advice to a Young Man: Now Is the Time to Prepare," *New Era,* June 1973, pp. 8-9.

3. **Ponder.** Check your dictionary and find out what *ponder* really means. If you aren't doing No. 2 above in accordance with No. 3, go back and start over with No. 1 again. This is a very important time in your life, so you want to get this right!

4. **Pray.** That's right. Pray again—this time for understanding.

5. **Mark.** Either mark on these very pages those items you now feel are most applicable to you, or prioritize them on a separate list you can keep handy.

Now for the smorgasbord I promised you.

The Appetizer—Mission Presidents Speak

What are the areas in which new missionaries have most often not adequately prepared?

London: Too many have a great difficulty in being able to read and write, and unfortunately even more in knowing how to spell. Many have not learned to study. Few have an awareness of what the Holy Ghost is, how he operates, and how to receive a spiritual witness. Many have not borne testimony until the time of their missionary farewell. Some have never faced reality in making a real commitment to anything.

Montevideo: Missionaries need a knowledge of the scriptures and a good system of how to study them.

Oakland: Too many missionaries arrive convinced that they do not have a testimony when in fact they do have, though it might be a small one that needs some work done with it. Too many have never really been told that a mission is a lot of hard work! They need more teaching experience, more experience in understanding the nature of the Spirit.

New York: Too many missionaries lack understanding of the importance of personal righteousness and discipline and the need to be totally honest with themselves and with others, especially their bishops and stake presidents.

Paris: A missionary should prepare in five basic areas: learning obedience, sacrifice, hard work, prayer, and faith. Faith makes the impossible possible and opens closed minds and doors. Until he learns to understand and walk by faith a missionary is not very effective. He should understand that a mission is hard work and requires giving up thoughts of cars, girls, music, and home. He should be willing to give these eighteen months *everything he has.*

The Main Dish

There are a variety of offerings that follow that may or may not be an area you need to chew on for a while and digest carefully.

Lost opportunities. President Christensen of the MTC says there are a lot of people "who kick themselves after they get here [at the MTC] saying, 'I wish I'd taken advantage,' or 'I wish I'd paid more attention in seminary,' or 'I wish I'd had more opportunity to learn so I could be as far ahead as some of my companions are in their scriptural understanding or their understanding of the gospel.' Some have worked with the scriptures and are conversant with them and some are not. Sometimes it's because they have just been reactivated in the Church. Sometimes it's because they're new converts. Sometimes it's because they were negligent. They were around, they were in the Church, but they took it less seriously."

The flashback syndrome. Brother Kenneth W. Godfrey, former president of the Pennsylvania Pittsburgh Mission observed that when his missionaries requested an interview it was usually because of the "flashback syndrome." Did you know it's absolutely impossible to remember something you haven't seen or heard? You can't recall filthy language or a dirty joke if you haven't heard it. Nor can you have a "flashback" experience of a pornographic picture or an R- or X-rated movie unless you've *seen* one. Unless you've experienced an immoral act, Satan can't possibly bring it back to your memory no matter how much he might like to. Brother Godfrey says it was his experience that "young men who lived riotous lives tended to have flashbacks in the mission field. They would hear a song in a shopping mall, or something else would happen that would cause them to relive a bad experience. This had a devastating effect upon them spiritually and almost 100 percent of the time they would talk with me about it and tell me how much spirituality they had lost. They came to the conclusion that even though repentance is real and a great cleansing factor in our lives, it is still better never to have sinned."

Satan enjoys most throwing in a flashback when you are most diligently struggling to "get the Spirit"—at critical times during your mission, or during your courtship, or when you're blessing your children. But he just can't do it unless you have provided him with something he can make you remember. So be smart . . . take it from those who have gone on before. Avoid not only evil, but even the very *appearance* of evil (1 Thess. 5:21-22). Don't allow the "flashback syndrome" to ever be a tool Satan can use against you!

The dumb club. Often a missionary looks back at high school and/or college with a little remorse and wishes he had changed certain patterns of behavior because of the adverse effect he can now see that it has on him in the mission field. He becomes an unhappy member of the how-could-I-have-been-so-incredibly-dumb club. For instance, are you one of those who has some of "those kind" of pictures secretly hidden somewhere in your drawer, usually under your socks and underwear—where you didn't think that Mom would know about them, but she really does? Hmmm? Dumb! You're giving Satan a foothold to use against you later at a time of his choosing—a foothold he cannot possibly obtain without your help! Dumb.

Brother Robert Swensen, Director of Pre-Mission Services for the Church, observes that there is often a fine line between pranks that are just pranks, and pranks that can cause some real problems for their perpetrators at a later time in their lives. "There are foolhardy pranks—the toilet papering of a friend's home and such. Those kinds of things are not particularly going to get you in trouble and would not stop you from going to any particular country on your mission, although it's another habit that you're getting yourself into that could become a negative factor. The other kind can get you arrested. Shoplifting, for example, is considered by some as just a prank of sorts. You do it on a dare. But if you get arrested, then you have a police record, and that will show up when you want to go on a mission. The same is true with drugs, including marijuana. Certain countries make it a matter of policy not to issue a visa to anyone who has a police record. A prospective missionary could be limiting where he might be called to serve because of a few previous experiences some young people think are harmless."

Maybe your bishop and your quorum advisors really know what they are talking about after all!

A parole officer told me that a good number of states will "book" a person for shoplifting. That means being fingerprinted, having "mugshots" taken, and being entered on a police record with both local and federal authorities. "Jobs, scholarships, missions, military service, and many other hopes and goals can be affected. To some kids it might seem funny somehow, but when a young man is arrested, none of his friends is smiling anymore. In some states you are guilty of the crime even if you're only *with* a person who is shoplifting and *your* parents can be liable not only for what your *friend* stole, but also for the store's costs for security patrols, and all legal, attorney, and court costs. At that point, nobody's laughing anymore."

Representing the Savior as one of His missionaries can be a pretty scary proposition in and of itself. Complicating your life with silly decisions that lead to needless hassles because of some dumb dare or prank that really proves nothing is anything but wise. If you've made some mistakes, let your bishop and the Lord help you. In other words, repent *now*, then go thy way and sin no more! If you've been wise enough not to have fallen, I'd like to give you a pat on the back and say "Good for you, my brother!"

In either case, remember His promise: ". . . but if ye are prepared, ye shall not fear." Every missionary worth his salt will smile and tell you that's true, that's true, that's *true*.

Now, do it!

The Dessert

Our actions are determined by our attitudes and desires, which in turn are the result of our thinking process. How important it becomes to control our thoughts! Learning to exercise total control over your mind is an exhilarating and Godlike experience.

President Grant Von Harrison explains it this way:

"Attitudes and desires are formed as a direct result of what we think about. When a person chooses not to use his free will in directing his thoughts, he leaves the dimensions of the mind that control his desires wide open to suggestion. If we do not make an exerted effort to control and direct our thinking, our desires and attitudes will be influenced primarily by the adversary, other people, music, movies, T.V., radio, newspapers, etc. So you have the choice of deliberately directing your thinking, or allowing other forces to dictate your desires and attitudes. We are responsible for our thoughts." (*Drawing on the Powers of Heaven.*)

Some Helpful References

1. "Before the Call," David R. Mickel, *New Era*, March 1982, pp. 14-18.
2. Grant Von Harrison, *Drawing on the Powers of Heaven* (Provo, Utah: Ensign Productions, 1979).

7
GETTING READY: A PRACTICAL GUIDE

How about a little self-evaluation? Check the appropriate squares in the following chart:

	Constantly	Weekly	Monthly	Occasionally	Rarely	Never
Do you have:						
Difficulty getting along with others?						
A feeling that people are not fair?						
Loss of temper?						
Overwhelming stresses and tensions at home?						
Thoughts about suicide?						
A feeling that people don't understand you?						
Hopeless discouragement about school or work?						
Hurt feelings?						
Preference to be alone?						

We'll come back to the chart a little later. If I've guessed right, it's started you thinking a little, and that's good.

Let's refer back for a moment to President Kimball's 1973 article in the *New Era:*

> It is incumbent upon each person to prepare himself [to serve a mission] . . . in three areas:
>
> 1. Keeping his life clean and worthy and remaining free from all the sins of the world.
>
> 2. Preparing the mind and the spirit—to know the truth.
>
> 3. Preparing to finance his mission so it may be his own contribution, so far as possible. (p. 9.)

With the Prophet's suggested triad for prospective missionaries in the back of my mind, I talked to several men with a wide range of experience in this area. Comments from just three of them follow.

Let's imagine that you could have an interview with your branch president at the MTC six months before you arrived there. What suggestions do you suppose he might offer to help you avoid the mistakes he's seen so many others make?

I discussed that concept with President Paul R. Warner who has been a branch president at the MTC. I asked him first what a missionary's biggest surprise is when he enters the MTC. He responded, "It's the immediate *total* immersion in gospel activities. For most missionaries to eat, sleep, drink, think, ponder, play, and do everything on a gospel-oriented basis is quite a surprise. They are more accustomed to riding up and down Main Street, honking the horn, dating the girl friend, going to shows—all of a sudden that's all gone."

What does he suggest that prospective missionaries do differently?

"Start using appropriate language! Don't be so eager to please the crowd. The language that is so common in the locker

Getting Ready 65

room, especially for the fellows, can be very damaging. I would encourage them to use language appropriate for a Latter-day Saint. And I would encourage them to get their prayer habits together."

What about the young men who are struggling to come to terms with themselves, who don't feel they have acquired that "spark" in their heart, that strong testimony?

"In many cases," President Warner says, "that spark, that testimony, that commitment is developed right at the MTC. As long as an elder comes in clean and with a desire to gain a fuller testimony, he'll be glad he came because he can catch the vision. It's an exciting thing to witness the miracles that happen at the MTC. Commitments, inner healings, attitude changes, the desire to do good, the evaporation of worries over girl friends—all these things occur because the desire to serve the Lord becomes paramount."

As you might suppose, President Joe J. Christensen of the MTC has some excellent suggestions relating to five distinct areas: (For more of his ideas see the June 14, 1980 issue of the *Church News*.)

1. **Savings.** Any missionary who has done all he can to finance virtually his entire mission from his own savings is a truly dedicated person. Missionaries like this come into the MTC with great spirit and enthusiasm. While in the field they are very conscious of being sure they don't spend more than is really necessary. They have a sense of purpose and know the value of money and many other important things. Obviously it is not the most impressive indication of one's personal responsibility to a mission if he owns a car and a stereo and yet expects the ward or other people to support him on his mission. Each should do all he or she can.

2. **Gospel understanding.** Without question the missionaries who have the greatest amount of success are those who have a strong commitment to and understanding of the gospel. As one elder said, "It's very difficult to teach anything

you don't know." Prospective missionaries find real strength in learning and being able to locate the sixty-six basic scriptural references that are used in the missionary discussions.

3. **Language study.** For years the First Presidency has encouraged parents and children to enroll in language classes. Those who have studied a language are generally much better able to speak English than those who have not. One man has said that you never really know your own language until you've studied another language. Generally speaking, missionaries do a lot better at the MTC and in their mission language experience if they have studied a language during their school years.

4. **Social graces.** If there is ever a time when someone should be on his absolute best behavior (including good manners and etiquette), it is during that time when he represents not only himself and his family, but also the Lord in missionary service. How to dress, eat, speak with good grammar, and conduct oneself appropriately in the presence of ladies and others of all ages are all very important to know. It takes more than a month or two to learn these skills.

5. **Testimony.** And then, of course, the most important, the *sine qua non* (the "without which not") of missionary work, is testimony. Any missionary who has a real testimony will hang in there when the going gets tough. He knows why he's here in the ultimate sense. And so anything that can be done to build testimony is a real blessing. A deep commitment needs to be developed so that when problems come up, missionaries are not easily moved off base. A testimony is an anchor. It's the most important thing for a missionary because it's the spirit that converts people.

President F. Wayne Chamberlain of the Canada Calgary Mission says, "The 'average missionary' requires four to five months to make the transition from self-centered John Smith to 'turned-out' genuinely-interested-in-others, spiritual *Elder* Smith. I believe that any missionary who will follow these twenty-one suggestions will save three to four months of this transitional adjustment as he begins his mission."

The twenty-one steps he itemizes have been used by a number of other mission presidents and prospective missionaries with great success during their last weeks at home.

1. Read the Book of Mormon at least three times (once during the final thirty days).
2. Read the New Testament, Doctrine & Covenants, Pearl of Great Price, *A Marvelous Work and a Wonder, Jesus the Christ,* and *Articles of Faith.*
3. Memorize the first discussion (Restoration) completely (and the second, if possible).
4. Pray vocally ten minutes both morning and night for three months.
5. Attend three or four temple sessions, minimum.
6. Split off with the full-time missionaries assigned to your area once each week during the last three to six months.
7. Bear testimony weekly in some way to a nonmember during the last three months.
8. Slow down dating, or stop for the last thirty days. Avoid being *alone* with your date.
9. Repent and confess all iniquity to your bishop. Control your thoughts.
10. Turn off car radios and home stereos during the last two weeks.
11. Fast (for specifics) twice during the last thirty days.
12. Omit sex-oriented movies, movies with coarse language, rock concerts, and dances.
13. Rise at 6:00 a.m. and retire at 10:30 p.m. for sixty days. (D&C 88:124.)
14. Study scriptures and discussions one to two hours

per day for sixty days, from six to eight a.m., if possible.

15. Learn buying, cooking, and ironing from your mother.
16. Develop a ten-minute exercise program and follow it for thirty days.
17. Read the Joseph Smith story four times.
18. Ask the "golden questions" daily for thirty days.
19. Write your personal testimony in six copies of the Book of Mormon and give them to friends.
20. Obtain your patriarchal blessing after fasting for twenty-four hours.
21. Begin your missionary journal thirty days prior to your departure. Record your feelings.

In addition, President Chamberlain encourages becoming familiar with three key missionary scriptures:

2 Nephi 32:3—"Feast upon the words of Christ; for behold the words of Christ will tell you *all things* what ye should do."

D&C 88:63—"Draw near unto me and I will draw near unto you."

D&C 4:5—"An eye *single* to the glory of God qualify him for the work."

Now you've read some very specific suggestions from three very good men. It would be beneficial for you to read this chapter again. Then take these suggestions to your Heavenly Father in holy prayer, and ask Him to further enlighten your mind as to the specific areas that are most applicable in your particular situation. Then make a plan, and *act* upon what he has told you. Remember the trilogy: Do it. Do it right. Do it right now!

Oh, yes—that little survey you filled out at the beginning of this chapter? You'll be filling it out for real when you send in your personal missionary recommendation form. Review your answers again, and if you see any apparent weaknesses or areas that you feel would be worth working on, why don't you make them a part of your plan, too? Do it!

8
THE SUCCESSFUL MISSIONARY

"All men are born equal, but some outgrow it."
—Anonymous

"I would give all of my wealth, and all of my worldly possessions, if I could have a positive assurance and knowledge that I would know my loved ones after death and that they would know me." Thus Elder Alvin R. Dyer quotes a wealthy industrialist. Elder Dyer then goes on to say,

> It is my observation that men are thirsting and hungering for this knowledge . . . . The youth of the Church, as were their parents before them, are of noble birth, having been in the pre-existent presence of God. It is up to them to fulfill the purpose of their earth-life existence by adhering to the standards which they know to be true. They should prepare themselves for leadership in the Church and in life by appropriating God-given principles of truth. If their preparation is complete and they are ready . . . (*The Challenge* [Salt Lake City: Deseret Book Company, 1962], pp. 104-105.)

Well, why don't you complete that sentence? He's writing about you, you know. Are you willing to pay the price to become a truly successful missionary? To be the bearer of that knowledge that so many are hungering and thirsting for? Can you suggest a better return on your investment of eighteen months of your life?

There will be no one during your mission who will be more involved in helping you succeed than your mission president. He and his wife will be doing everything in their power to meet the needs of each missionary who is entrusted to their stewardship. When you first meet him, you will probably be impressed with his understanding and patience. It was Elder Paul H. Dunn who said that "being a mission president . . . is like taking two hundred priests on an overnight hike for three years." So be ready to become acquainted with a very special man.

Let's look at what just five of our mission presidents have noticed about successful missionaries:

Mission Presidents Speak

London:
1. They have learned to work.
2. They have developed a positive mental attitude.
3. They desire to be of service to others.
4. They are on a mission for the right reasons.
5. They have developed an attitude of optimism and happiness and can see the good things in people rather than just their feelings and faults.
6. They know what is in the scriptures.
7. They have spent some time away from home and have learned to get along without getting homesick.
8. They usually have not come directly out of high school, but have had some work

Getting Ready

and higher education experience so that they are a little more broad-based.

9. They are obedient to the commandments of the Lord and to the mission rules and regulations and don't try to fight the establishment.
10. They lived worthily before they came.
11. Their speech and personal habits are above reproach.
12. They have learned to keep themselves under control. They do not engage in masturbation.
13. They have a testimony of the Savior.

Paris: 14. They are self-starters and motivators.
15. They love the people.
16. They avoid contention by learning something from each companion.
17. They love to talk to their Father in Heaven and do it often during the day.
18. They have faith the Lord will direct their efforts if they will set goals. They literally call down the powers of heaven in their work.

Oakland: 19. They are willing to work and willing to learn.
20. They are willing to follow the program.
21. They are willing to work to make their testimony grow.

Montevideo: 22. They have the ability to love their companion and people in general.
23. They have a strong testimony.

New York: 24. They have come prepared with a know-

ledge of the gospel.
25. They have learned to love the Lord.

(How do we learn to do that? It always comes back to the same thing: *keep the commandments.*)

How many of these twenty-five traits do you already have? How many would you like to have? Remember the plan we talked about in Chapter 7? Is there anything you'd now like to add to that plan?

Two Keys to Success

Missionary work is never more successful than when two certain elements are put to good use. Those two elements are a *good attitude* and the *Holy Spirit*. As a matter of fact, there is hardly a problem in any area of our lives that can't be resolved when these two elements are working in combination with one another. Neither one of them alone will be as effective as when they are combined. The combination will work miracles. I *know* that's true!

A good attitude. You've had the privilege of being in the presence of someone who consistently radiates a positive mental attitude. It's a pure delight to watch them function and to feel some of those good vibrations rub off onto you, isn't it?

Perhaps you've read of the prolific statistics relating to Wilford Woodruff's missionary service. (Preston Nibley, *Exodus to Greatness* [Salt Lake City: Deseret News Press, 1947], pp. 301-302). One habit stands out above all the rest as a symbol of his good, positive attitude. Often the first thing he did upon entering a new town was to look for or prepare a suitable pond for the baptisms he expected to perform. He knew he was there on the Lord's errand and fully expected to be blessed by the Lord for his efforts. Ponder for a minute and let that marvelous bit of positive mental attitude sink in. By the way, have you ever noticed whose name the administration building at the MTC carries?

The Holy Spirit. In the mission field the "senior companion" to our friend "positive mental attitude" must by all means be the Holy Spirit. Does this passage from the Doctrine and Covenants make you tingle as it does me?

> ". . . Ye elders of my church whom I have appointed: Ye are not sent forth to be taught, but to teach the children of men the things which I have put into your hands by the power of my Spirit; And ye are to be taught from on high. Sanctify yourselves and ye shall be endowed with power." (D&C 43:15-16.)

I hope you realize what the Lord means when he promises "and ye shall be endowed with *power.*" Decide for yourself what is involved when the Lord commands us to "sanctify yourselves." Once you've got that concept nailed down to your satisfaction, make it No. 26 on your list, and then *do* something about it!

Let's explore for a moment the vast power of the Holy Spirit. One of the fundamental callings of the Holy Ghost is that of a *testator*, which is why we so often find ourselves coming under the influence of the Holy Ghost when our efforts are directed toward testifying of the truthfulness of the gospel. "Wherefore, I the Lord ask: unto what were ye ordained? To preach my gospel *by the Spirit,* even the Comforter." (D&C 50:13, 14, italics added.)

Harold B. Lee has explained that a testimony is when your heart tells you something that your head doesn't necessarily understand. I like that.

Prime ministers and kings and their worldly realms will come and they will go, but once you've heard the voice of the Spirit—well, nothing else needs to be said. You just *know*, and after that, nothing else even comes close.

May I share with you now, my special friends, a small excerpt from my missionary journal?

Monday, May 20:

> This evening . . . for the first time in my life [I] heard very distinctly the *whisperings* of the Spirit. Now, I've felt inspiration before, and have, I know, been inspired to say or do certain things through its influence. And thus I've been able to appreciate, albeit on a pitifully *small* scale, how it is that the Brethren can guide and direct the Church through divine inspiration. But what I witnessed tonight was a direct and undeniable manifestation of the spirit. . . . I have heard *The Voice.* I cannot deny it, nor would I have the desire to try to. I know that Christ lives, and that his Holy Spirit directs and communicates with his messengers as the need arises. I called on him tonight in a moment of confusion as to what answer should be given to an honest question by Pastor Visani, and the answer was whispered to me in my mind just as unmistakably as had Elder Stokes whispered the answer in my ear. I'm still pondering the wonder of it all.

That same sweet definite Spirit came to my assistance on a very regular basis after that. Often the Voice would come at a time or in a way that could, if followed, have lead to probable embarrassment or, in doctrinal terms, to the "fear of men." Paul H. Dunn relates an experience wherein he had to overcome this "fear of man" when prompted by the Spirit.

> "In our final days in Boston as our mission was drawing to a close, we were having an open house, and Billy Casper was kind enough to be our visitor to teach non-members.
>
> One day before the meeting I was standing in a line at the bank to close out our account. As I stood in line, I thought, 'Whew! Ten minutes to relax.'
>
> Then the Spirit prompted me, 'Paul, warn your neighbor.'

I thought, 'Oh, I am so tired!'

But the Spirit reminded me that I had been sent out for 1,095 days to warn thirteen million people.

Then I asked, 'Who is my neighbor?'

The Spirit replied, 'The guy in front of you.' (Too often we warn our neighbor next door to death, but our neighbor is also the fellow whom we do not know.)

So I tapped this man on the shoulder. He turned around and said, 'Yes?'

I asked, 'Pardon me, sir, do you happen to be a Mormon bishop?' (Since he had a thin cigar in his hand, I didn't think he was.)

He said, 'No, I'm not a Mormon bishop. Why do you ask?'

I replied, 'I hope this isn't offensive to you, but you look like one.'

He asked, 'What does one look like?'

So I described a Mormon bishop.

This man was a sharp-looking young executive, thirty-five and well-dressed, and he seemed to know what he was doing and how to do it. When I finished describing a typical Mormon bishop, he said, 'Well, thank you. I didn't know I projected that well.'

I replied, 'You really do.'

We moved up a couple of spaces, and then I asked, 'You play golf?'

He replied, 'I'm a Sunday hacker.'

'What's your handicap?'

'Thirteen.'

I asked, 'How would you like to reduce it?'

'Well,' he replied, 'who wouldn't?'

I said, 'Do you know Bill Casper?'

'The golfer? Yes, I've heard of him,' was the reply.

I said, 'I've got him coming to a meeting tonight. Would you like to meet him?'

He said, 'Believe I would.'

So I took a card out of my pocket and wrote the mission address on it. Then I said, 'You're my guest tonight. Seven o'clock.'

That night when he arrived at the mission home, I introduced him to Billy Casper, and he thought that was great.

We had a tremendous meeting that evening, and before he left, I said, 'You would not be offended if I had two young men call on you to teach you more, would you?'

He replied, 'I'd be honored.' He was baptized ninety days later—without the cigar. And he is going to be a great leader one day." (*Discovering the Quality of Success* [Salt Lake City: Deseret Book Company, 1976], pp. 25-26.)

The Spirit often trusts missionaries to respond only after spending a great deal of time and effort setting up a perfect situation. We've all heard innumerable accounts from missionaries about being impressed to go to "just one more" house, or walking down "that street" instead of this one or the other one, or sensing a burning need to begin a conversation with a particular person, as Elder Dunn was prompted to do. I, too, am a humble and grateful member of that club. I remember the first time it happened. Here's how it's recorded in my journal:

Saturday, April 20:

The young Chavez boy arrived—very tired after a full day's work, but with his baptismal clothes tucked carefully under his arm. His baptism was a thrill to watch. He came up out of the water with his face filled with joy. It was after he changed clothes and was confirmed that he shared with us the full story of such a spiritual conversion. "For the last four years I have earnestly searched," he explained, "investigating many churches, but never finding the *full* truth in any. A little discouraged, I decided that if I was incapable of finding the true church of God, then I would plead to the Lord to bless me that His church might find me, and to this end I directed my prayers. It was the following day that you and Elder Hill knocked on my door, and had you simply proclaimed yourselves true ministers of Christ and challenged me to baptism, I would have been so impressed and inspired by such a direct answer to my prayer that I probably would have accepted baptism on the spot." A beautiful smile spread over his face, and then he sealed his testimony with his tears. As it was, I had not been impressed to challenge him until our *second* meeting, which taught me that I should repent and try to stay in better tune with my Heavenly Father and do better the next time. What a beautiful experience that locked all our hearts together that special day.

Imagine what might have happened had we not been attuned to the impression to knock on his door that day. I would hate to even think about the possibility. Wilford Woodruff, because he was attuned to that endowment of power, was once led to an opportunity to baptize over six hundred souls—which would not have happened had he failed to follow the Voice which, by his own account, asked him to do something that seemed totally illogical at the time. (See Leon R. Hartshorn, *Classic Stories from the Lives of Our Prophets* [Deseret Book Company, 1975], pp. 120-122.)

Story after story can be told of allowing the Spirit to lead missionaries. Can we expect anything less when we read 3

Nephi 4:6: "And I was led by the Spirit, not knowing beforehand the things which I should do."

One more story from my own mission: I received a rather desperate telephone call one day from a neighboring branch. The mission president was planning to attend the baptismal service scheduled at this little branch, and was bringing as a guest the General Authority who was the supervisor of all South American missions. Since the branch was located in a beautiful little seacoast resort town, a photographer from the *Deseret News* was also coming to photograph the baptisms to be performed in the bay there. However, all the baptisms had fallen through, and so the presiding elder had suggested that the visiting brethren continue up the coast to the next little seacoast town so they could take their baptismal photographs there.

That sounded fine, except the next little resort town was ours, and we had absolutely no baptisms planned at all. I asked him to please call mission headquarters back and tell them not to come since it was such a long trip and there was nothing for them to come for. He agreed that that made a great deal of sense, except that they had already departed. So there we were with the brethren coming to join us in our baptismal service and us without anyone to baptize. What to do?

We decided to inquire of the Lord.

Sunday, December 30:

> It was like no other prayer I've ever heard. Four elders of Zion went down on their knees side by side and humbly each one . . . offered up his soul, and poured out his heart. Looking back on it now, I think it would have been pretty difficult for the Lord to deny a prayer and fast such as had been dedicated to His work. And when President Fyans and his guests arrived at our branch that afternoon, the Lord had seen fit to arrange for the baptisms of five eternal souls.

Elder McPheters and I had the privilege of performing the baptisms in the beautiful blue waters of the bay at Punta Del Este on that bright, sunny day. How marvelous to see the hand of the Lord involved in such a personal way as a man, young Carlitos Pallas, and a woman and her two children entered the kingdom of the Lord that day. The photographer said he had a glorious time, taking pictures to his heart's delight. The spirit was beyond description. And these things come forth by nothing, but by prayer and fasting.

An interesting footnote to this story is that a few months later my father wrote to say that my mother was sure she had seen my picture in the *Improvement Era*. He teased her about it because the picture shows only the backs of two missionaries with a little boy standing between them just before his baptism. Out of the many thousands of missionaries in the field at that time, my father felt it wasn't very realistic to suppose the picture could have been of me. But she insisted that a mother can recognize her son's back anywhere. You know how mothers are.

When I wrote back I told her I wasn't aware of any picture of me in the *Improvement Era* (May 1963). But then a few weeks later our branch received its copy of the magazine, late as usual, and sure enough, there were Elder McPheters and I getting ready to baptize little Carlitos that beautiful summer day on the beach. The picture had gone throughout the Church and had been used at the New York World's Fair as a symbol of missionary activity in the Church. When we saw it, it represented much more than that—it was a living, visual symbol to us that God not only answers prayers, but takes a very personal interest in the activities of his missionaries.

So now you know the story behind the photograph found at the front of this book. One thing you may as well learn right away is that you can never fool your mom. You know how mothers are.

9
I'LL GO WHERE YOU WANT ME TO GO

"Boise! Can you picture me in Boise? Of course I told them no!"
  (*Debbie: Diary of a Mormon Girl,*
                      Act II.)

Have you ever wondered about the procedure that determines which missionary is assigned to which mission? Do computers determine how best to fill the staffing needs in each of the more than one hundred and ninety missions? Can you imagine human beings trying to make the best decision when it involves so many tangibles such as how to most effectively preach the gospel in over fifty languages throughout eighty-two nations, territories, and possessions? What about such intangibles as the 30,000 missionaries to be assigned, each with his own individual strengths, weaknesses, and other variables that make up the complex and highly unpredictable human psyche?

Actually neither computers nor human beings are in control, although both contribute greatly to the assignment-making process. The answer is that the Church is run by the rock of revelation—the arrow still goes down, remember?

Let's take an imaginary trip with your missionary recommendation form.

It will arrive with the approximately 350 other recommendations received by the Church each week. Each is reviewed for completeness by the Missionary Department and is then sent along for consideration by the Church's Missionary Committee, which is the Quorum of the Twelve. Of this number, three have been called as the Missionary Assignment Committee. They are Elder Mark E. Petersen, Elder Bruce R. McConkie, and Elder Thomas S. Monson. The Missionary Committee, through the executive administrators, administers the Church's missionary program.

Those in attendance at the Tuesday morning Missionary Assignment Committee meeting are one of the three members of the Twelve mentioned above and two members of the First Council of the Seventy. In this meeting each missionary recommendation is prayerfully considered. The meeting lasts as long as it takes to give each missionary recommendation personal consideration.

The recommendations are then sent to the President of the Church for whatever action he wishes to take. When President Spencer W. Kimball makes the final determination, a letter of call is sent out over his signature to the missionary.

President Loren C. Dunn, formerly managing director of the Missionary Committee, has told us that "the calling of a missionary in The Church of Jesus Christ of Latter-day Saints is carefully designed to allow for the inspiration of the Lord and to provide the help and assistance necessary so each missionary can succeed in his calling. For the past five years I have had the opportunity of sitting in the weekly meeting where missionaries are recommended, subject to the final approval of the President of the Church. There are instances, too numerous to mention, that clearly demonstrate that these young prospective missionaries are called of God by inspiration." (*New Era*, June 1973, pp. 10-11.)

Getting Ready

Brother Robert L. Swensen supports Elder Dunn's testimony of the part inspiration plays in determining where a missionary is to serve the Lord. As the Director of Pre-Mission Services, your missionary recommendation goes first to his desk for clearance. He then assists the Missionary Assignment Committee by presenting your recommend for assignment, and duly records their decisions. "I've seen probably eighty or ninety thousand missionaries receive their calls. Several times a month assignments are made that from a logical standpoint might seem completely wrong, but from a spiritual standpoint end up completely right. I have no question but what these calls are all inspired."

I remember when Steven Carlston was anxiously preparing for his mission call. He was an excellent athlete and was particularly well known in our area as a basketball star. "I'm not really concerned about which mission I'm called to," he told me, "but all the fellows on the team are nonmembers. They all think I'm crazy to give up two years of my life to a church—especially with the prospects of playing college ball right around the corner. For their sakes, it would be nice if I were called to somewhere that sounds a little glamorous. It doesn't really matter to me, but I feel it might help them be a little more receptive to what I've decided to do."

Guess where Elder Carlston was called? Pocatello, Idaho. Serving as his elders quorum president at the time, I received a letter from him after about two months in the field. You should have heard his excitement after just a few weeks of dedicated work. "Did you know this is the second highest baptizing English-speaking mission in the Church?" he wrote. "I feel so sorry for so many of my friends in other missions who can't find anybody to teach. How disappointing that must be. I sure know why the Lord sent me here. This is the neatest mission in the world!"

And I'm sure it was. Isn't that great? Incidentally, I ran into Elder Carlston a little while ago. I asked him to recall some of his feelings now that he's a family man and has had a few years to reflect on his life and on his call. Here's what he had to say:

> As a youth I followed in my father's footsteps of inactivity in the Church. Consequently, the friends I associated with were not members. Most were athletes, cheerleaders, class officers, and generally people classified as the "in crowd." Most of them had no idea I was Mormon because I never mentioned the Church, hardly ever attended, and had no friends in the Church.
>
> As my testimony began to grow because of continued prayer, I began wanting to tell others of the Church and its truthfulness. I still avoided telling my friends, however, for fear of being snubbed as a "born again" or "Jesus freak."
>
> After hearing President Kimball speak in general conference in April of 1974 I knew that I must share my testimony by serving a mission. As I discussed my plans with my friends they realized my commitment and respected my efforts and decisions. However, I was considered a bit strange to give up two years of my life in such a manner.
>
> They all wanted to know where I was going on "this mission thing." I could only tell them that I wouldn't know until I received a letter from Salt Lake. They suggested that since I was paying my own way I ought to be able to choose where I wanted to go instead of arbitrarily being told where I would go.
>
> I hoped from the day I sent in my papers that my call would be to an exotic, exciting place far away, perhaps England, Japan, South America, or even better, South Africa. I wanted my friends to be impressed.
>
> As I waited for my call, I looked through books on different countries, trying to feel some inspiration

as to where I might be called. I even suggested in my prayers that a foreign country would be nice.

Then as the day for my call drew nearer, I began to feel the Spirit touch my heart, saying, "Steven, wherever the call is is where the Lord needs you and where you'll grow the most." I became absolutely converted to the fact that my call would be inspired.

When the long-awaited envelope arrived, I sat down with my parents to open it. My father asked, "Where would you like to go?" I answered quickly, "South Africa!" Then my mother asked, "Where *don't* you want to go?" I answered just as quickly, "Never to South Dakota or Idaho!"

As I began reading the letter, the Spirit spoke once again, saying, "The call is from God, be happy!" I then read that my call was to the Idaho Pocatello Mission. My heart pounded with joy. Both my parents thought I was joking, but when they read the letter, they were speechless.

Everyone tried to console me, including my stake president, but I was feeling great about my call. I knew it was from God, In spite of this I still felt uneasy about telling my friends. A call to South Africa would have been "cool." Idaho was definitely not "cool." Yet once they knew, they accepted it, and everyone asked me to send them a bag of potatoes.

After serving for only a few months, I could see the Lord's wisdom in sending me to Idaho. I wouldn't have wanted to serve anywhere else. The opportunities to teach and baptize on a frequent basis far outweighed the momentary thrill of telling my friends I was going to some exotic location.

Another good friend recently returned from a great mission in the Netherlands. He even had a baptism—one baptism! That seems like such an awful lot of effort for just one baptism. But in addition to the beautiful concept the Lord teaches us in Doctrine & Covenants 18:15, do you really understand the eternal implications inherent in one baptism?

Suppose you have the great privilege of baptizing one person, and that person converts his or her spouse, and they have four children born in the covenant. Then if each of them converts a spouse, and have four children each, and so on, by the time your original baptism is a great-grandfather or a great-grandmother, there will be over one hundred of his or her descendants in the Church. Within the next seven generations, well over one million people could be in the Church because of your original one baptism. At that rate it would take only six more generations to equal the population of the world today.

I wonder where the Lord has in mind for *your* mission?

10
LOOKING FORWARD TO THE MTC

"In these latter days—as we work toward fulfillment of ancient and modern prophecy—there is a greater need than ever before for more and better prepared missionaries. To fulfill this need is the purpose of the Missionary Training Center."
—Spencer W. Kimball

A special feeling is present in the halls of the consecrated building. You sense it the first time you're here, as you notice the walls lined with life-sized pictures of missionaries in action throughout the world, as you witness the dedicated activity of the missionaries temporarily living here. Everyone seems in a hurry to be going somewhere important. Yet, everything is in order. Organization and a sense of purpose permeate the atmosphere and its hard-working, motivated inhabitants. It just feels good to be here.

I won't attempt to take you through the various activities you'll experience at the MTC because an outstanding booklet has been prepared just for that purpose. It can be requested at no charge from the MTC or the Church Distribution Center. (*The Missionary Training Center*, PTM18219.)

What I will attempt to do in this chapter is to let you read about the experiences of those who have gone before. They are the real experts, and they can tell you better than anyone what is waiting for you here and what you can expect to find.

"This is quite a place. You wouldn't believe the spirit that's here. One of my sensei (teachers) said the temple has a great spirit, and second only to that is the MTC. I believe him. It's great."

"I don't believe I have constantly felt the spirit for as long as I have felt it here in the MTC. The missionary spirit is catching, and it's super. My companions are really great. You really learn to love each other as you grow in the knowledge of the gospel together."

"I really do love it here. There is truly a spirit here that is so constant and so strong that one would have to be totally hardened against the Spirit to *not* be able to feel it. Learning is made much easier through the help of the Man upstairs. It's great to be here."

"We have three excellent teachers, but our night teacher is especially good. He says he's going to see that every one of us succeeds, and I believe him because he's working our tails off, but it's what we need."

"Each day we have gym for an hour. They have us do exercises, and then we can play basketball, volleyball or work out with weights. Even for gym we are working hard."

"Having a General Authority come to speak once a week has to be one of the highlights of this place."

"Today in our Sunday School class we talked of Joseph Smith. The testimony of his mission burned in me. I could not hold back the tears. The Spirit was so strong not just for a minute or two, but for an hour. If I could live my life worthy to feel that spirit constantly throughout my life, I would feel worthy to meet my Maker. I love it here at the MTC."

"I think I have done more praying these past seven days than I had my past entire life."

"I'm having no trouble at all here at the MTC except for one thing that I just can't understand. Why does the time here fly by so fast? I've been here five weeks, and next Saturday I get my flight plans to leave. There are reasons that I wouldn't mind staying here for a while longer, but bigger and better reasons say, 'Get to Japan.' I really feel good about being here, and I'm loving every minute of it."

"Well, here we sit discussing how we've all changed in the two short months we've been here. We've all grown up so much. I've learned to overlook people's shortcomings and learn from their strengths. I've learned that all we can do is work hard and then be happy with it. I have learned many things, but most of all my testimony has grown."

"Living at the MTC is like living at the temple. You can make the MTC experience just as great or miserable as you wish, but for me I consider those two MTC months to be two of the greatest months of my mission."

Allen C. Ostergar, Administrative Director of Training at the MTC, writes:

> There are two great purposes for sending missionaries. One is to search out the people who are looking for the truth and bring them into the Church through baptisms. The second great purpose of missionary work is to provide missionaries with the experiences that will bring them close to the Lord and prepare them to serve in other capacities in the Church.
>
> Everything we do at the MTC is directed at helping the missionary develop spiritually by those who have the spirit. We also hope to be able to give them some skills and knowledge that will be helpful to them as they do missionary work. One of our goals here is to help each missionary experience four principles personally that we hope in turn they will apply as they interact with investigators: respect, confidence, trust, and love.
>
> The experience that the missionaries have here at the MTC is one that would be extremely difficult to duplicate anywhere in the world; and if it could be duplicated, it would come only at great cost. The miracles that occur at the MTC could only

Getting Ready

happen within the Church of Jesus Christ.

Living at the MTC may be the missionary's first extensive stay away from home, but everything he does there is designed to help him grow without having to experience the growing pains so often associated with being "on his own." Elder Vaughn J. Featherstone talks about growing pains in his book *A Generation of Excellence.* Of the ages of sixteen, seventeen, and eighteen he says:

> These are the years . . . when he begins to reach out beyond himself and have confidence. These, too, are the preparatory years that the Lord so wisely provides for a boy prior to his mission call. During the years of seventeen, eighteen, and nineteen there comes, too, a restlessness of spirit which prompts desires to cut the apron strings and leave home. Thus a mission call at nineteen seems God-given: it comes at the absolute crest of life when a young man needs the almost limitless opportunities of growth, of testimony building, of self-discipline, of learning to work, of spiritualizing his life. (Bookcraft, 1975, pp. 103-104.)

The Missionary Training Center's statement of purpose touches on those very needs and starts the missionary on programs that will meet them.

Many missionaries feel the need to express their feelings directly to President Joe J. Christensen as they leave the MTC. He shares a few excerpts from those letters:

> "I especially want to take time to express the appreciation I feel for the gracious courtesies you extended to my parents. They were profoundly impressed with the MTC and especially with Presi-

dent Jensen. They are not yet taking the discussions, but I am sure that with the help of our Heavenly Father the seed that has been planted will eventually result in a harvest of a temple sealing for our family."

"I'm awed by the love within the MTC. I've learned a lot more than just Chinese! I can honestly say these past few weeks have been the happiest, most inspiring weeks so far."

"Our stay at the MTC is finished as of today. Before we left we wanted to let you know how much we've enjoyed this last month. It's been a growing experience in many areas. The programs here have been so helpful to us and the teachers have been fantastic. Never once did they say anything that discouraged us, but constantly worked with each of us, encouraging us to be great missionaries."

"I loved the MTC because of the Spirit I felt there and the time I had to prepare. Instead of fighting against the system and the spirit, I went with it. I became a missionary. I certified four days out and hit the field ready to teach anything. I had the confidence. The MTC gave me that foundation."

Part III

Parents and Girls Who Wait

11
WILL SHE WAIT?

> "Oh, Wally—I will *wait for you! If they should torture me with acid and leave me to die in the sun, I will still be* true!"
> (*Saturday's Warrior*, Act I.)

So vows the well-meaning but impulsive Julie in the airport farewell scene of *Saturday's Warrior*. Then, after the plane has departed and she turns to leave, she just can't resist the temptation to check out some very cute boys who happen to be walking by.

Is she wicked? Evil? Or at the very least, unforgiveably disloyal?

A little while ago I heard a girl named Becky mention to a friend that she hadn't heard from *her* missionary for three weeks, and she was beginning to worry that maybe he had forgotten her! Her terminology confused me, so I asked, "Did you say *your* missionary? Why, Becky, I had no idea *you* had a missionary. Did you know that Heavenly Father has some, too?" She began to grin so I teased her a little more. "Gee, that must be neat. What does he preach, the gospel of Becky? Imagine *having* your very own missionary!"

Becky quickly corrected me. She didn't really mean that *she* had a missionary but that he really was Heavenly Father's. And do you know that's true? Girls don't *have* missionaries. Heavenly Father does.

Should a girl "wait" for a missionary? Should *your* girl wait for *you*?

Personally, I dislike the connotation involved here. For example, what does a girl do when she "waits" for a bus? Or in a long line at the supermarket? For a dentist's appointment? Basically, nothing. See what I mean? If a boy really *loves* a girl, is that what he wants for her? An area in her life where she is expected to experience no growth? Is that what Heavenly Father would want?

When I attended Ricks College, we knew of a group of ostensibly sincere young ladies who had banded together to form a club. To be a member, a girl had to "have" a missionary. (There's that term again. Doesn't that sound awful? "Have a missionary? No thanks, I just had one.") One of the rules in this club's constitution said a member was dropped from the club if she dated other boys during the two-year waiting period because that showed she wasn't "loyal." These club members told me they usually held their meetings during homecoming dances and on prom nights when they sat around and shared pictures of "their" missionaries, read each other's letters, and cried a lot. They tried to come up with reasons why they should feel good about avoiding opportunities for social growth.

The girls adopted a Hebrew name for their club: *Shomrah Hai-el*, which they stated translates roughly into English "Forever Faithful." On campus a popular biology teacher with an infamous sense of humor dubbed them instead the "Organized Stagnation Committee." Of the two names, most folks seemed to prefer using the latter, so it stuck.

I asked President Joe Christensen of the MTC this question: "If you could counsel with the young men who have girl friends a few months before they enter the MTC, what kind of arrangements might you suggest they consider?"

He advises:

> I would prefer that a missionary come [to the MTC] without a serious attachment to a girlfriend. That's mainly because they don't have the worries at home, they're not divided in their attention, they can focus on their mission *totally*. I recognize that situation doesn't always exist. But if they are a few months away from their mission and they have an option of whether to really get involved with somebody in a serious way or not—I say *don't*. They should make a conscious decision not to become involved seriously. Date several girls and have an enjoyable social time. But don't get tied down to any one kind of commitment.
>
> However, I realize that does happen. But even in cases where it has become serious, I still think it's better not to have a formal engagement. If they do, then there's always a little more tension.

And who needs more tension?

Girls who wait for missionaries may find that the relationship resembles this illustration upon his return:

Start vs. **Return**

Somehow I don't think this is what Heavenly Father really has in mind. A far better technique than "waiting" is what I call "supporting." What a tremendously positive relationship *that* can build into. Both of you growing in healthy, positive ways, becoming the kind of young man and woman each could be interested in on a forever basis is an admirable goal, but one to be taken care of at a time especially set aside for that is definitely not during your mission. Remember that special part in your mission call that says "leaving behind all other personal affairs"?

So what is involved in "supporting" a missionary? Let's be realistic. Picture yourself battling the adversary twenty-four hours a day. Satan has been trying all day long to get your mind away from the Lord's work without success. Can you see yourself coming home after a hard day's work in the field? You smile as you find a letter waiting—and it's from her! You sit down and what do you suppose you read? Let's go to my file and look at the following, adapted from an actual letter received by one of our missionaries:

Hi, Sweetie!

> Gosh, Ricky, I love you so much. I just want to hold you and love you and be with you always! I got two cards from you today. They're so beautiful, Rick. I love it when you send and write really sentimental things. That poem you wrote is so neat.
>
> Right now I'm at the Johnstons' watching Mork and Mindy. It's so special. Remember the night we watched this together at your house? That was so fun. I can't wait to share more memories with you. I love you, honey. Bye for now.

Where do you suppose your mind is at this point? Do you think you are contemplating your sacred missionary calling, or do you think this seemingly well-intentioned young miss has you thinking instead about memories of her and *her* needs and interests? Unfortunately, at this point she has more to say:

I just got home from the library a little while ago. And I just got through arguing with my mom and my sister, and I don't even know why. Ricky, I feel so terrible, so awful. I really need you. I want you so badly. I'm really lonesome. The girl I went to the library with is Vickie. She was engaged to a guy who was in the Navy. Well, everything fell apart. He came home and nothing worked out. I can't help but think about us, Rick. I'm so afraid. I'm so scared that you'll come home different, and you won't feel the same towards me. I'm so scared, Rick. I'm really upset now, and I can't stop crying. I love you, and I want to marry you. I really do. I know you need my support while you're on your mission, and I'll give you all I can. But I need yours, too, so desperately. I love you. I pray that everything works out with us. I'll do everything in my power to make it work. In your last letter you said you feel like there's somebody between us. What do you mean? Rick, I know I'm so demanding at times. I probably am a spoiled brat. I hope you never get sick of me. I hope you always love me. I know I'll always love you.

I think I've calmed down some now. Goodnight.

I love you.
Always,
Crystal*

The tip-off is in the last paragraph. Count how many of those sentences start with the word "I" or "I'm." It's part of an all-too-common syndrome among some of our young people today who think they're in love but are really only insecure. Strong, mature, eternal love never suffers from insecurity. But if she's "waiting" for you, she might be tempted to want you to

---

*Adapted from a letter obtained from the Missionary Emporium, Orem, Utah.

think about *her* needs instead of what you both know you really *should* be thinking about while you're on your mission.

So what should the girl who is happily "supporting" a missionary want to include in her *supportive* letters to you? Good question. She should think first about *you*. It really makes no difference if she's a mom-girl, a sister-girl, a friend-girl, or a girl friend-girl. She should consider the impact her letter has on the young man who receives it.

One elder advised: "Come to the mission field in your letters, rather than trying to bring us home to you." How is that done?

Encourage friends to send letters that (1) strengthen your testimony; (2) make you feel good about being in the mission field; and (3) encourage you to strive to increase your skills and effectiveness while laboring diligently in the Lord's vineyards. For example,

"Dear Elder:"

(Notice the majestic strength of this great title! It says so much more than "Hiya, Big Jeff!" or "Dear Timmy.")

>"I just came from the neatest testimony meeting, and I want to share some special feelings with you that I gained there. I was particularly impressed when Sister Linda Clark talked about how her family had recently grown so much closer together. She said. . .
>
>"There was a very special thought on the bulletin board at the Institute. I copied it so I could share it with you. It said . . .
>
>"Remember Brent Youngberg, who bragged he'd never go on a mission? Well, his farewell is next Sunday. He's really happy; he said the change for him came when . . .
>
>"A beautiful new family was just baptized in our ward; the Bedingers. It was so interesting to hear them tell of how they first came to know of the gos-

pel. They said it all happened when the missionaries . . .

"Do you know how proud I am of you and the wonderful job you're doing there? If the people in your mission field only knew how very lucky they are that they have Elder Jeff Anderson there to teach them. . .

"Keep up the good work, Elders!"

Now how would those comments make you feel? Happy to be in the field.

I know you can't tell people what to write, but you might be sure that Mom and other special friends have an opportunity to read this section. They may also want to check out an article called "What to Send to a Missionary," in the June 1973 *New Era*.

I asked a mission president in Canada about how he feels when a new elder comes into his mission who has a commitment to a girl friend back home. Without hesitation, he said, "I figure they lose about four to six months off the front of their missions before they can start being effective, and maybe not even then can they do as much as they could without the girl friend hanging on them." Isn't that sad? The sweet young thing at home thought she was doing the right thing by promising to "wait" for "her" missionary. But is she really helping?

Oh, I know there are exceptions—some of them very good ones. Jessie Evans Smith (wife of the Prophet Joseph Fielding Smith) used to gently remind girls that the one thing they could count on was that if someone was married when he returned home, it wouldn't be *him*.

And incidentally, no discussion of supporting a missionary would ever be complete without mentioning one of the most appreciated international symbols of support for the modern-day missionary, sometimes also referred to as *chocolate chip cookies*.

Mission Presidents Speak

What differences might you expect in a missionary who is committed to a girl friend at home as compared to those with no such commitment?

Oakland: This can work for either good or evil. A girl who is supportive but insists that her boyfriend keep his mind on his work and reach his potential can be a positive influence. Those who write too frequently or too lovingly of many things at home serve to distract the missionary and keep him from getting his mind on his work. It does not help to have a girl friend tell a missionary how much she misses him. It would be far better to have her tell him how proud she is to have him on his mission and be interested in his investigators, his convert baptisms, his companions, the programs of the mission, and so forth.

London: Often they have a financial strain put on them because they want to buy things for their girl friend to remind her that they still love her and that she is the one, and they spend money they do not have just to make an impression on her.

Paris: A missionary who is committed to a girl at home usually has a harder time losing himself in the work than one who is not committed. There is so much lost time in letter writing and most of them lose the girl friend before they get home anyway. The girl at home so often by her lack of understanding writes things that discourage the young man rather than encourage him.

New York: We immediately have new missionaries read President Kimball's classic talk to missionaries, "Lock Your Heart." Until they learn to bring their heart into the mission field, which I think means their affections, I find that they limit their ability to progress spiritually. I have also found that those who are committed to a girl friend at home have a very difficult time bringing their mind into the mission field.

Montevideo: The missionary who is committed to a girl friend has problems adapting to the mission, while the one who has no such commitment generally has already passed the test of dedicating himself to the work and focusing totally on the work.

A few final thoughts from Elder Loren C. Dunn of the First Quorum of the Seventy:

Three questions could well be asked: (1) Will waiting be good for the person at home during the time when dating and social activity should be a prime part of a young person's life? Is it appropriate for a young person to avoid such associations for a two-year period of time? (2) Will waiting be good for the missionary? Does having a girl who is waiting at home cause the missionary to become preoccupied with thoughts of her? In order to be successful a missionary must serve the Lord with all his "heart, might, mind and strength." Does the girl who is waiting encourage that kind of loyalty to the Lord, or does she unwittingly cause a division of loyalty? (3) Will waiting be good for the missionary work? If the missionary suffers, then the work suffers. Certainly every Church member will want to do all within his power to help missionary work succeed, and the way missionary work succeeds is for the missionary to succeed.

Some missionaries have told us that sending tapes may well create problems. To actually hear the voice of the girl friend will often develop feelings of homesickness and cause the missionary to become diverted from his work. For the same reason it is recommended that family and friends should not telephone the missionary in the field except in dire emergencies. (*New Era,* April 1974, pp. 9-10.)

12
A MATTER OF FAITH

> Many of you young women say, "What will I ever do if he leaves me?" So you hold him back. You allow your association with him to go beyond where it should. You often contribute to his decision not to serve. You sometimes even contribute to his unworthiness to serve . . . . Let him go. Not just let him go, but encourage him. . . . You can make all the difference. Help keep him clean. Help him to be prepared. (William R. Bradford, October 4, 1981 General Conference.)

When I entered the mission field in Uruguay as a fresh, new nineteen-year-old, I noticed a number of elders had girls "waiting" for them. They were easily recognized because of the large 8×10 glossy photos peering at them from their desks, much as one might display a trophy. Often I observed that a considerable part of their day was planned around what one mission president terms as "the most subtle false god in the mission field—the mail box." Unfortunately, this fact often placed investigators and other pertinent missionary work in a second or third place on the missionary's priority list.

So it was with considerable interest that we listened to Elder A. Theodore Tuttle address us at an all-mission conference, especially when he chose to direct a portion of his talk to those among us who had girl friends at home. His counsel was full of love and good sense, but he shot straight from the hip when he said:

> Brethren, do you really think that if you're diligently taking care of the Lord's business here in the mission field twenty-four hours a day, that he won't take care of your business at home? If you're doing what you should be doing as His missionary, do you really think he would let that special young lady marry someone else if she was actually the right one for you?
>
> You see, what it *really* comes down to is a simple matter of *faith*. Have you developed your faith to the point that you can simply trust Him to take care of your business at home? If so, then let's get to work on the business at hand here in the mission field and avoid losing so much of our time worrying about the girls back home. It's hard to be trunky in a cottage meeting; you don't get homesick in a baptismal font."

My, how I love that special man! His words caused a lot of us to reflect more seriously on our priorities. Serving the Lord in the mission field, we realized, was really the very best way for us to learn to eventually become loving, caring husbands and devoted, capable fathers. And isn't that what our girls really want? And it really does come down to a simple matter of faith in the Master, after all. I think many false gods were toppled that day.

Although not as common, nevertheless the same premise applies when a young man is "waiting" for a lady missionary. It is still simply a matter of faith.

I can't help but think, whenever I'm asked about missionaries and their concerns about the girl back home, about that powerful paragraph in the letter every missionary receives from the Prophet: "you will also be expected to devote all your time and attention to serving the Lord, leaving behind *all other personal affairs.*" As Brother Robert L. Swensen points out,

> And it doesn't say "except a girl friend." Isn't that plain and clear? The closing paragraph states: "Greater blessings and more happiness than you have yet experienced await you." My goodness, what you're doing by going on that mission is taking the Lord at His word; He's letting you commit Him, and by so doing you're guaranteeing for yourself greater blessings and *more* happiness.

It would be unfair, however, to suggest that a rule so general as that recommended in Chapter 11 should have no exceptions. Indeed, a number of very worthy examples come to mind. I want to share three.

Our former bishop, who was called recently to be a mission president, shared a very special relationship with his sweetheart, Judy, prior to his mission. After he accepted a mission call to Japan, Judy continued to date other young men, but also kept a scrapbook of the letters, momentos, and souvenirs Larry sent home quite faithfully. When he returned home after serving an honorable and very successful mission, Judy had grown, too, and their feelings blossomed to a very happy and rewarding conclusion. Appropriately, they sealed their vows at the sacred altar of the temple. Today, that scrapbook stands as a splendid reminder of those special days of growth in their lives. It's an important part of their family history. It's a tribute to their faith in the Lord and brings great joy to the family and friends who have seen it. Judy "supported" Larry in such a way that they could both grow from it.

In this second example, a mission president in England received a frantic call from a missionary whose companion had decided his mission was "too hard" and was at that very moment headed for the airport to return to the United States.

The mission president immediately proceeded to the airport, and succeeded in locating the young, homesick elder before the plane departed. He was able to persuade the elder to come back to the mission home to fill out the "necessary forms." The elder agreed to do so, but insisted that nothing would change his mind about returning home.

On the ride to the mission home, the mission president gave a sympathetic ear to the discouraged young man, and even encouraged him to talk about his home and the things that home represented to him. It was during this time of sharing that the missionary mentioned his girl friend, and how desperately worried he was about her well-being and who she might be going out with while he was gone.

The mission president was duly impressed that this was a very special young lady indeed. Upon arriving at the mission home, he went into a separate office and called her long distance all the way from England. Once she was on the line he told her who he was, that the young man she was writing to was in his office, and would she like to talk to him? After being assured that it would be appropriate in this case, she agreed. The missionary was then called into the office. The mission president handed him the telephone without indicating who was on the line and then discreetly left the room. Approximately fifteen minutes later a very subdued and pensive young elder walked out. Somewhat mellowed now, he sat down by his president, who waited patiently for him to speak. Finally, it came.

"President, may I stay?"

"Why would you want to stay, son? Has something changed your mind?"

"It's my girl, sir. I just wanted to go home so I could be

with her. But do you know what she said? She said I was copping out. She said I could come home if I wanted to, but if I was going to quit and give up on something as sacred and important as a mission, she really wouldn't be interested in seeing me when I got back because she couldn't see that we'd have anything solid enough from which to build a relationship. She said that the little boy in me was battling the man I was becoming; that I should stay here and become a man, and if I did, she would promise to keep writing to me."

"And is that what you want to do?"

"I knew all along it was wrong to quit. I guess I just felt sorry for myself, like a little boy would. But she's got a lot of strength. And I want to start working like I should so someday I'll become worthy of someone like her. I'd like very much to stay, sir."

And he did.

Thank goodness (literally) for the strength of that girl, that special, sweet handmaiden of the Lord who had the necessary strength when the boy didn't and would let him use some of hers when he struggled.

The third example comes from a former mission president:

> When we first had the privilege of getting together with the fine parents of the young returned missionary who had proposed to one of our daughters, we learned something that made us very proud. We had invited his family to our home and were discussing the wedding plans. Our daughter invited her fiance to assist her in the kitchen so that they might prepare refreshments.
>
> After they left the room, this father, who was a bishop, turned to me and with tears in his eyes and a quiver in his voice, said, "You know I'll be eternally grateful to Robyn. Curt was really undecided about a mission. One night he came home and said, 'All right,

Dad, I'm ready to go on a mission. I want to go; I *really* want to go.' Do you know what changed his mind? He had proposed to Robyn, and she had replied, 'Curt, my husband will be a returned missionary. And not *just* a returned missionary. He'll be a *good* returned missionary.'"

I hadn't known that until his parents shared that with me. Robyn and Curt had gone together before his mission, and during the courting he had proposed to her, and we never knew that. Then he went on his mission, returned, and they took up the courting again. That to me has been a valuable example of the influence a determined young lady can have on her future missionary boyfriend. She can *put* him in the mission field.

After all, it really *is* a matter of faith, isn't it. . . . ?

13
DEAR JOHN

He's just a friend . . . a kind, unselfish
boy who understands my pain.
(Saturday's Warrior.)

I've worked with a number of elders who have actually received their "Dear Johns" with considerable relief. For many of them the uncertainty, the frustration, and the helpless feelings all disappear once the letter comes. It provides such a relief that they can finally get to work with those good feelings of total dedication that they always wanted to have in the first place. Many have indicated that they didn't feel their missions really began until after the "Dear John" arrived.

Of all the "Dear Johns" I have seen, the most classic example was from the girl who ended up marrying the very person who—well, why don't I just let you read for yourself.

Dear John,

Howdy! So how ya been? I really did enjoy your last letter. What a crack-up! I must say, you are the letter writer.

Actually, John, there's so much I need to say, and I don't even know where to begin, so much has happened since you left. But first, let me say, or actually, have you noticed that this is a dear John letter and not a dear John? Oh, John, I'm hopeless; I guess the best way to say this is to just be blunt! You remember your "childhood friend," Sam? Remember how you introduced us at your open house and asked him to take good care of me and that you were leaving me in his care because you'd know I'd be safe. Well, John, I can assure you that he has taken *very* good care of me. He has kept me very safe and very secure. He has really done a good job in helping me be less miserable and has really helped me in missing you and trying not to think about us (me and you). He has been the best friend a person could ever want. He's a special guy. I can see how you two stayed friends for so long; you're so much alike.

John, I do love him dearly and appreciate you dearly for helping me find such a neat guy. In fact, John, I've become so attached to him, that I realize that there is no way I could live without him. You might say we have decided to insure our eternal friendship, enough to have it sealed for time and all eternity. It's so amazing how fast these things happen. You prepare so many years for this time in your life. John, it's such an exciting feeling to know you've found "the one."

John, I want you to know that you still hold a special place in my heart. I appreciate all that you've done for me. I have so many special memories of such tender moments. You've really helped to make my life full and helped me grow in so many ways. You're a special guy, and I will always remember you.

I wish you luck in everything and success throughout your life. May you find lasting peace and happiness in this troubled world.

I know you haven't been out long, and I'm glad this all happened before you were. Make it a good mission. Stay strong. You'll make it! You're a great guy.

> My prayers are with you,
> I love you,
> Sue

P.S. The Sam Hubbard family. Mrs. Sam Hubbard. Doesn't that sound classy? Has a certain ring.

P.S.S. John, don't worry, there's still Keri Maw, or Bearible Jones, or Patti Pickel, or even good old T. B. Breath.*

Ouch!

I guess that letter was necessary under the circumstances, but how do you suppose John felt about life when he finished that letter? How effective can a missionary be for the next part of his mission? It probably made him a better man once it finally came, but the terrible hurt and feelings of rejection and depression could have been avoided had a more *faith*-oriented (there's that word again) arrangement with Sue taken place prior to his departure. Boy, a "Dear John" can hurt!

On the other hand, he could have been like my friend, Royal Meservy, in Southern California. Royal asked ten girls to wait for him. That way each time he got a "Dear John" he said it didn't hurt as bad.

Missionary Funerals

How missionaries choose to handle these "epistles of

---

*Adapted from a letter obtained from the Missionary Emporium, Orem, Utah.

doom" varies from mission to mission, and the creativity of the elders who concoct ways of making a devastating experience into something that is almost bearable never ceases to amaze me. Sometimes, for example, funerals are necessary.

I transferred to a branch during my mission and arrived smack in the middle of one such funeral service. The missionaries marched in a slow procession, humming, in unison, the muted tones of the "death march." Each wore a "mourning suit," which most missionaries seem to have on hand for just such auspicious occasions. (These are also sometimes referred to as "rain suits," "ski suits," "diving suits," and "tents," the nomenclature varying from mission to mission.

In the middle of the procession two elders carried an 8×10 glossy photograph of the perfidious one, held, appropriately, face down. The victim, with a hood (dish towels) over his face, usually brought up the rear of the procession, while his companion led out, slowly strewing ashes across their path as they walked. When they reached their destination (a backyard incinerator), the picture was unceremoniously ripped into sixteen uneven pieces and set afire until nothing was left but bitter ashes. Then everyone present was happy to spit on the ashes.

I've seen numerous photographs meet their demise in this manner. Sometimes I've wondered if there was some sort of "reversal ceremony" should the miscreant write that she had changed her mind.

Mission Newsletter

When a "Dear John" arrives in the New Zealand Mission, the Elders forward it to the Mission Headquarters where it is reproduced for publication in the monthly mission newsletter, so everyone can enjoy it equally.

Placing the Face

Even more effective and almost as common a way to deal

with the arrival of a "Dear John" was to collect a girl's wallet-sized picture from each elder in the branch. All the pictures plus the wallet-sized picture of the former girl friend were then included in the following letter:

Dear Mary:

Thank you for your letter. Your name is familiar, but I can't place the face. Please remove your picture from the group and return the others.

Sincerely,
Elder Doug Meredith

The one thing all "Dear Johns" seem to have in common is an empty and somewhat helpless feeling at the end because of the traumatic way that things worked out. I doubt that this is what the Lord really intends our young men and women to go through as part of accepting a mission call. With a little more planning and preparation (not to mention *faith*), such heartbreaks could so easily be avoided.

The following letter, written by a missionary in the field to his sweetheart, is a classic in its own right. Of all the material I've used in lectures on missionary work over the years, I think I've received more requests for copies of this letter than any other item, and oddly enough, most of those requests have come from young ladies who have felt these same special feelings, but had difficulty putting those feelings into words. The letter portrays a great spiritual metamorphosis taking place in the heart of this young elder and is really what this chapter is all about:

Dear Lisa,

It has finally hit me! I can now see the vision of missionary work. I have got so little time here and there is so much to do. I need your help. I have spent too much time concentrating on things I shouldn't—marriage and schooling. Remember that poem I sent you? Let it go and if it comes back, that one? Lisa, you are going to have to let me go. And I will have to let you go, too. And if are meant for each other, then we'll come back forever.

I worry that this will make you sad. I know how sensitive you are. You should be happy because we are doing what's right. I am giving up things that are important to me now for other things that are even more important; I am preparing myself better for marriage because I am going to serve the Lord with all my heart, might, mind, and strength. Things will work out for the better!

Lisa, some missionaries can handle having a girl friend waiting but I can't. You are so blasted wonderful that I spend time thinking about you. This can no longer be. Only thoughts of my mission will have room in my head now. I am no longer thinking about home and school. This is not a "Dear Jane." I love you and want to marry you, but in my own due time. I am doing this for the both of us. I am preparing myself by giving my all. I've heard that a mission determines the missionary's life; that he'll never rise higher than what he did while on a mission. You wouldn't want to marry me the way I am now. I haven't risen very high, yet.

Lisa, please support me by loving me enough to let me go, pray for me, and help me. I am scared because I don't want to lose you, but I have faith that we'll "find" each other again. I'll be a new and better person. Right now I'm not the man in your patriarchal blessing, and I may never be. Lisa, look for that man—hopefully it's me, but right now it's not. Marry the right man as I know you will.

Lisa, I love you, I love me, I love God; that's why I'm doing this. Please let's keep in touch. I am interested in your life. Tell me the major events, and I'll write when important things happen, too. Good luck!

> Love eternal,
> Elder Layne Christensen*

---

*Adapted from a letter obtained from the Missionary Emporium, Orem, Utah.

14
MOM AND DAD

> Now they never had fought, yet they did not fear death; and they did think more upon the liberty of their fathers than they did upon their lives; yea, they had been taught by their mothers, that if they did not doubt, God would deliver them. And they rehearsed unto me the words of their mothers, saying: We do not doubt our mothers knew it. (Alma 56:47-48.)

You will probably notice, within a few weeks of your departure for the MTC, that your mother, and perhaps even your father, will begin to get a little emotional. It's a natural reaction and has nothing whatever to do with not wanting you to go. It's just that this is a very significant event in their lives as well as in yours. A former apostle who was sent on his mission to New Zealand at the tender age of seventeen once said,

> One of the greatest joys of my life is rubbing

shoulders with these young missionaries. I was a young one myself once, just a kid turning seventeen when either by inspiration or by audacity I was called to go out into the world. I went down there where they rub noses. The first dear old sister that rubbed my nose looked at me, and tears came down her cheeks, and she said, "Does your mother know where you are?" I said, "Yes, I think this is the first time in my young life that my mother really knows where I am." (*Matthew Cowley Speaks*, [Deseret Book Co., 1954], p. 275.

Parents at this time feel a strange mixture of pride, anxiety, overwhelming love, and sadness mixed with delight. It can be explained, but only with great difficulty! I've heard one mother describe it as that "miserable joy."

It has been my observation that among the happiest missionaries are those who (1) have developed a positive attitude about their missions, and (2) are fortunate enough to receive warm and *appropriate* support from a family who cares. Parents—particularly first-time missionary parents—as well as prospective missionaries, may be unsure of how to provide that appropriate support.

I've asked several people who have served in key positions in the Church missionary system about their ideas regarding the most beneficial relationship parents can foster with a missionary son or daughter. Brother Paul R. Warner, who served as a branch president at the MTC, had some helpful comments:

Parents should:

1. Encourage their children to fully confess their sins to their leaders so they can be whole before leaving home.
2. Help sons and daughters to develop a positive attitude about rules and regulations.

3. Lead the prospective missionary to experiences with the scriptures. A missionary should not be a stranger to the standard works.
4. Lead the prospective missionary to experiences with the Spirit by having times at home when the Spirit touches his life.
5. Demonstrate that life is not meant to be negative, overwhelming, or depressing, and that they can laugh and smile. Missionaries need to know that life is fun, good, and positive. With that attitude, they know they are going to be able to make life more valuable to others.

Mission Presidents Speak

London: Parents should provide adequate funds for missionaries to be able to do productive missionary work. Work out a reserve so that the missionary is not always on the thin edge or worrying about where his funds are coming from. At the same time parents should not send more money than the missionary needs. A budget session before the missionary leaves for the field is well worth the time and trouble. The missionary son or daughter should know how to prepare and live by a budget. Parents should not visit their son or daughter in the mission field, and in general, should let their son or daughter come home from the mission field rather than going to pick them up. Limit the sending of packages to Christmas time and birthdays.

Paris: Parents should encourage and receive reports on the missionary's success and progress. Parents need to follow up on their missionary and his obedience. They very often help their son or daughter slow down at the end of their mission by reminding him of how much time he has left and how glad they will be to have him home again. This should be avoided.

New York: Many young people have never been counseled by their parents because the parents seem to rely on priesthood leaders. Parents need to talk with their children regarding personal righteousness.

Communication between home and the missionary is carried on almost exclusively in letters. In addition, all mission presidents had something to say about letters and what should and should not be in them:

Oakland: Don't write too often or too infrequently; write regularly (once a week). Don't talk as much of home as you do about what is happening to the missionary, the missionary programs, his investigators, what is going on in the mission field. It does not help to tell of fishing trips, hunting trips, things that make a missionary homesick. When missionaries have trouble with a companion, ask them to evaluate themselves and suggest ways to improve the relationship such as a good inventory session, prayer together, study together, and perhaps even a fast for their companionship. Do not automatically side with your son or daughter.

London: Do what you can to "go on a mission" with your son or daughter rather than trying to "bring them home" in your letters. Address missionaries as "Elder" or "Sister" rather than by their first names. Write about what is happening in the Church, messages you've heard in meetings, ideas on missionary work,

> things that direct the missionary's attention toward more effective missionary work. I would have an arrangement where the missionary did not call the parents on the telephone or the parents the missionary, except in extreme, dire emergency.
>
> Montevideo: Be consistent in writing once each week. Maintain love and harmony in the home and convey this to the missionary. He needs to know what is going on at home, but parents shouldn't write about all of their difficulties in detail. I have found that nothing helps like support from home.

President Gordon B. Hinckley also emphasizes the importance of the kinds of letters missionaries receive:

> "To be effective a missionary has to move away from home; so the kind of mail he receives will make a vast difference in what he does and how he feels. Letters that set forth the problems at home, that dwell on the difficulties, hurt the morale of the missionary. Wise letter writers will be sure to state their positive feelings—how proud they are to have a missionary in the field, how the Lord is blessing them because of his work in the ministry. Such letters bless the life of a missionary." (*New Era*, June 1973, p. 32.)

Few parents will need to be reminded to pray for their missionaries. It seems to come automatically to them. After all, parents place one of their greatest treasures in the Lord's hands during the time of your mission—you! It's only natural that they will pray constantly for your health, safety, and success. And you'll be able to echo the sentiments expressed by Zelma Miller in the following:

> I have often wondered
> As the weeks go by,
> How my footsteps were guided

From time to time.
Who turned the wheel
When I knew not why,
And took me away
From the way I planned?
Who led me up
To an unknown door,
With a familiar message,
"Would you like to know more?"

Today came the mail,
With letters of cheer
From friends and relatives
Far and near.
I read them all
And then I knew;
For each one ended;
"We pray for you."
(*Especially for Mormons*, vol. 1, p. 256, 1972.)

One of my favorite stories for parents was told so beautifully by Elder Jacob de Jager; the story of the rescue in the storm. It involves a nineteen-year-old and a very worried mother:

> A ship was in distress, and a rowboat went out to rescue the crew. . . . The waves were enormous, and each of the men at the oars had to give all his strength and energy to reach the unfortunate sailors in the grim darkness of the night and the heavy rainstorm. . . .
>
> But the rowboat was too small to take the whole crew in one rescue operation. One man had to stay behind on board because there simply was no room for him; the risk that the rescue boat would capsize was too great . . . . But the same crew could not make the second trip because they were exhausted.
>
> So the local captain of the coast guard asked

for volunteers to make a second trip. Among those who stepped forward without hesitation was a nineteen-year-old youth by the name of Hans. . . .

When Hans stepped forward, his mother pannicked and said, "Hans, please don't go. Your father died at sea when you were four years old, and your older brother Pete has been reported missing at sea for more than three months now. You are the only son left to me!"

But Hans said, "Mom, I feel I have to do it. It is my duty." And the mother wept and restlessly started pacing the beach. . . .

After a struggle with the high-going seas that lasted for more than an hour (and to Hans's mother it seemed an eternity), the rowboat came into sight again . . . . The captain of the coast guard . . . called vigorously against the storm, "Did you save him?"

And then the people lighting the sea with their torches saw Hans rise from his rowing bench, and he shouted with all his might, "Yes! And tell Mother it is my brother Pete!" (*Ensign,* November 1976, pp. 56-57.)

As Elder de Jager says, "You never know whom you will save. It may be the one that on life's billows is tempest tossed, or it may even be the one that had been reported missing at life's sea."

In my file I keep a little note sent by a cherished friend of mine to his eldest son. It is full of love, and typical fatherly concern; but, notice the tender nuggets of wisdom from a father to his missionary son:

Dear Son—

You'll probably read this on an airplane headed for Japan. I can feel the knot in your stomach and the lump in your throat. You may even think there is an ache in your heart. But there is something else there. It's been growing since you were set apart: a love of God and of the people in Japan.

It won't matter that your love of the Japanese people will be tested by rejection. God won't reject you, and He will take you to people who will love your message, and love you. And you will lead them to love Him.

I love Him, and you,
Dad

At Our Son's Farewell

Here we are sitting on the stand, looking out over a congregation filled with so many friends and family. The thought crosses my mind that we as a family are being given a glimpse of what heaven will be like as we look into the loving faces and feel the warm spirit radiating from those in attendance. As the prelude music is played, I find myself wrapped up in flash backs of so many wonderful experiences we have shared with our nineteen-year-old son. From the trauma and joy of his birth to his first day at school, first little league game, junior high years (I could have done without the seventh and eighth grade years), graduation from junior high and into the choice high school years, which were filled with so many exciting and growing experiences. His first date to his last prom; his new letterman's jacket to his last game, and of course all those great friends who have walked through our doors during these many years.

Yes, I am tired; the last three months since receiving his call have been busy ones, filled with buying trips, doctor and dentist appointments, interviews, parties, father and son chats, and just trying to tame a lion. It's hard to believe it's finally here. I feel like we have been shaping, molding, and modifying a rocket for blast off, and the countdown is about the begin. Here we go!

I'm so proud of my wife and family as each one has participated on the program. Our son developed the program outline by himself. I guess that it's now time for me to speak. Okay, from the heart, Dad. What a joy!

Son, it's now your turn. Is this our son up there speaking with such conviction and so forcibly bearing testimony? I wish we could take all the credit, but we can't. Thank you, Heavenly Father, for his good friends, relatives, advisors, teachers and coaches who have all helped in bringing him to this moment. I haven't been looking forward to singing that closing song, "Til We Meet Again," but you know it wasn't too bad because this young Elder is ready and anxious to begin a new chapter in his life.

Next stop, the MTC. However, before then, additional choice experiences to be shared, setting apart counsel from a great Stake President, family get togethers, last minute visits by numerous friends, that last dinner consisting of eight courses, each of which was our son's favorite prepared by his loving Mother, packing the suit cases (he's going to need a companion just to help carry his luggage), and lastly, the great opportunity to place my hands on my son's head and give him a Father's blessing. What a choice experience through the power of the Melchizedek Priesthood to dedicate my son to the service of our Heavenly Father and through that Priesthood asking our Heavenly Father to bless and comfort him and to help him be an instrument in His hands for spreading that beautiful joy which each one of us are so grateful for.

Well, it's time to go, everybody in the car; we don't want to be late. As we drive down to the MTC, this is one last chance for us as a family to discuss past family experiences that we have shared over the years. Time for Mom to cover her concerns (for I believe the hundredth time) the importance of good eating habits, the importance of keeping your clothes neatly pressed and clean, keeping your room clean, staying warm, and write every week or I'll break your arm when you get home.

Here we are, everybody is so congenial and kind as we enter the MTC. Smiles are everywhere. The orientation was well done with sincere empathy for all of our feelings. Now it's time for that miserable joy I have heard so much about. Say goodbye, what a son. It's time for you to be on your way. We love and support you with all of our hearts. As he walks out the door, I find myself offering a silent prayer of gratitude for this my mortal son, in whom, I am well pleased.

As we travel home, minus one, there is a sweet spirit in the car. We had desired so earnestly as parents that the experiences of our son's call would be positive and beneficial to others, especially our other children and our son's wonderful friends, hoping that all that came in contact would feel the spirit of missionary commitment and purpose as he prepared to serve his Father in Heaven. Goodbye, my son. Now at last your mother will always know where you are.

EPILOGUE

ep'i·logue, n. 1. a speech, short poem, or the like, addressed to the reader after the conclusion of a work. 2. A concluding section, as of a novel, serving to complete the plan of the work.

My special friends—since you now know what "it" is all about, there's really only one thing left to say:

Do it!

Do it right!

Do it right now!

God bless you, my brothers and sisters, to follow your hearts, that you may experience the exquisite joy that comes from being led by the Spirit, I pray, in the name of Jesus Christ, Amen!